£1,

"

GW00374404

TRAIN TO JULIA CREEK

Also by Scyld Berry

CRICKET WALLAH

TRAIN TO JULIA CREEK

A journey to the heart of Australia

SCYLD BERRY

HODDER AND STOUGHTON
LONDON SYDNEY AUCKLAND TORONTO

To my father Francis Berry
And friends who have helped

The quotation from T. S. Eliot's 'East Coker' is reproduced by permission of
Faber & Faber Ltd.

British Library Cataloguing in Publication Data
Berry, Scyld
    Train to Julia Creek
    1. Railroads—Australia
    2. Australia—Description and travel—1981–
    I. Title
    919.4'0463   DU105.2

ISBN 0 340 33380 4

Contents

Acknowledgments

My thanks to Railways of Australia for their kind assistance.

Illustrations

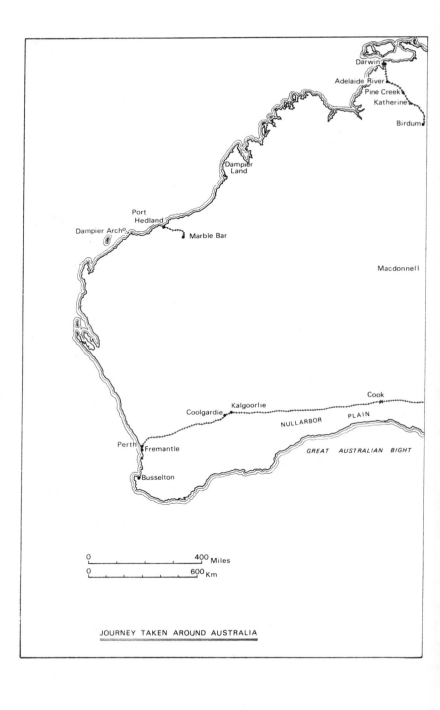

Darwin
Adelaide River
Pine Creek
Katherine
Birdum

Dampier
Land

Port
Hedland
Dampier Arch°.
Marble Bar

Macdonnell

Cook
Kalgoorlie
Coolgardie
NULLARBOR   PLAIN
Perth
Fremantle
GREAT   AUSTRALIAN   BIGHT
Busselton

0   400 Miles
0   600 Km

JOURNEY TAKEN AROUND AUSTRALIA

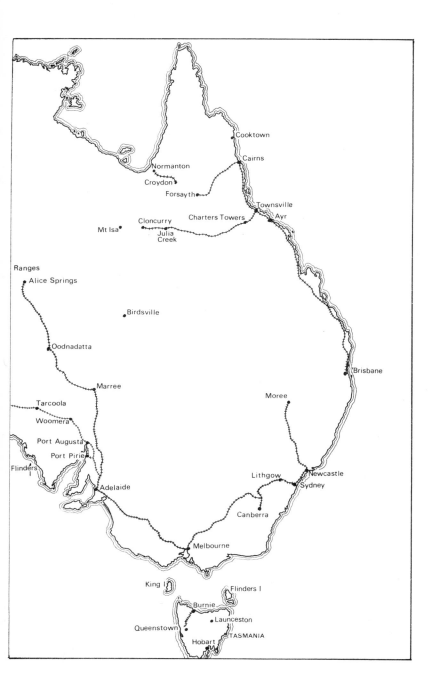

Introduction

Most journeys begin in a chair, if not by your own fireside then perhaps that of a doctor or a dentist. You sit and stare through the clear upper pane of his window at the blueness above, while the drill or doctor hums and traffic rumbles in the street below. At that moment the idea of escape crystallises, the first preconception of what is to come.

This particular journey started in a different kind of chair, ten years ago in Kuwait. I enjoyed several months of being 'affiliated' to the university there, the first time I had lived abroad, and at Christmas the Anglican chaplain was kind enough to invite me – as one of few unattached foreigners – to stay with his family. On Christmas morning I started on a paperback that he had on one of his shelves, Nevil Shute's *A Town Like Alice*: the gruesome story of an Australian crucified in Malaya for stealing chickens from Japanese officers, and of the English girl in a sarong who was forced to watch.

Christmas lunch came. And, wonder of wonders in a Muslim country, with it a rare bottle of red wine from the diplomatic allowance. Turkey was served, as hot as the afternoon; the bottle of burgundy waited upon the sideboard. We ate the turkey, wine-less, then the pudding, wine-less. It was not until the meal was being cleared away that the chaplain exclaimed: 'Good gracious! We've forgotten the burgundy.' Not all of us had. But by then it was too late.

Instead, therefore, of a mellow Christmas afternoon dozing in an armchair, I sat and read the second half of Nevil Shute's novel. It is almost another volume, the sequel about the girl discovering that the Australian, Joe Harman, had in fact survived and her going to Australia to find him. All works out, they marry and settle down in a Queensland outback town which they intend to make like Alice Springs ('a bonza town is Alice').

Arabia, where I was, seemed to have parallels with Australia, where I hadn't been. Desert or semi-desert dominates them both; the rains are everything; and this hostility of environment has engendered in both their peoples a code of generosity towards fellows and friendly strangers which strikes me – an inhospitable Englishman – as particularly admirable. Staring out of the chaplaincy window in Kuwait, I wondered what Alice Springs would be like, and also another place the book often mentioned, Julia Creek, the railhead to which Harman drove his cattle to load them on the train, way out in the Queensland bush. The name – feminine in a masculine country, soft amid ruggedness – stuck in my mind as some inconsequential but lovely-sounding names do, and there it stayed for ten years.

In that period, I went to Australia three times, enjoying the cities at first and their vitality, but after a while wanting to see something more. One friend, a journalist who divides his time between Sydney and Melbourne, said that he had always done the trip by plane, except once during a strike when he went by car. That's the temptation, because the two main airlines are quick and efficient, if not cheap. People are confined all too easily to the main cities on the country's periphery (the 'five teeming sores' in A. D. Hope's infamous phrase) and air-capsuled between them.

So on my fourth visit I was not going to be confined, but decided instead to travel round the country by train. It's not that I ever had anything more than a schoolboy's interest in railways, and many Australians, like that journalist, never travel by them. But any country populated by English administrators, Scots engineers and Irish navvies is going to have an extensive rail system, and the map showed that it penetrates places still not reached by sealed tarmac road – Alice Springs, for example, is not connected to Adelaide except by dirt track and railway.

Australia is the sixth largest country in the world, twice the size of India, and from Ayers Rock in the Red Heart the sea is over a thousand miles away in any direction. It is so sparsely populated that if the fourteen million Australians were uniformly spread out, there would be half a mile's distance from one to the next. No wonder perhaps, given its hugeness and dryness and flatness, that the geographer R. T. Maurice remarked: 'One who would travel this country for pleasure would go to hell for a pastime'. But I did not feel the same, and precisely because of its immense natural austerity, it attracted me greatly.

I began where Englishmen first began in Australia, in the north-west – not in Broome, the old pearling port, where travel-writers now U-turn their four-wheel drives in the wide main street and set off for a photo-feature – but in Dampier in the region of the Pilbara where two private railways operate: one is the longest private line in Australia, the other has the heaviest regular freight trains in the world. From there, my rail journey would describe a squared-off 'W' shape: from Perth to Adelaide, north to Alice Springs and Darwin, then to Tasmania for a holiday (it is now known as the Holiday, not the Apple, Isle) then up the east coast through Melbourne and Sydney into the Queensland bush, to end – why not? – in Julia Creek.

Julia Creek, as it turns out, has a population of 300 people, no more than in the day of Joe Harman. Originally, it was a pub where Cobb & Co. stopped with their stage coaches on the trail from Townsville to Cloncurry. It has a dirt airstrip, on which the Flying Doctor landed from Cloncurry to make his first rescue back in 1928. Julia Creek also marks the northern limit of sheep in Australia, and there used to be multitudes of them, but when the cost of hiring shearers pushed up to a prohibitive level, cattle were brought in. The local rule of thumb now is one cow for every seven to eight acres and one sheep for every three acres, but during drought the land cannot support even that low density.

How the town acquired its name has not been firmly established, I believe, until now. The relevant department of the Queensland government in Brisbane can offer no explanation of its origin. One local theory is that it was named by Donald McIntyre, a landowner, after a friend of his, an English actress called Julia Matthews. However, according to the mine of information in Julia Creek (Mrs Dawes, who used to run the post office like Flora Thompson in Candleford, following the goings-on in the town for half a century), a letter exists or once existed on the subject, written by McIntyre. In it he disclaimed the title of being the namer of Julia Creek. The creek (and, after it, the town) was almost certainly named in honour of Julia Matthews, but by someone else; someone, it transpires, eminent in the life of Australia.

Robert O'Hara Burke was an Anglo Irish Protestant from County Galway, who emigrated to Australia in 1853. Burke was impulsive, daring, cavalier – just the right kind of fellow to have around in the officers' mess of the cavalry regiment which he first joined, but hardly the painstaking, methodical man desirable for leading expeditions. Nevertheless, the Exploration Committee of the Philosophical Institute of Victoria chose him as leader of the expedition which they were putting together in 1860 for the purpose of 'traversing the unknown interior'. And Burke accepted the position, in part because of his love of one Julia Matthews, a dancer, soprano and actress. 'Leadership of the expedition,' according to the *Australian Dictionary of Biography*, 'was probably Burke's last chance of achieving distinction in his own, the world's and the divine Julia's eyes.'

Julia Matthews, who had been born in London in 1842, was taken to Australia by her parents at an early age. When twelve, she made her stage début in Sydney and went on to join a light opera company touring the Victorian goldfields. There, at Beechworth, she is reported first to have attracted Burke. In January 1854 Burke had been appointed senior police inspector at Beechworth but he did not stay long: he heard about the Crimean War and dashed off to Europe, only to arrive – perhaps characteristically – too late. He returned therefore to Beechworth and in 1858, when Julia was sixteen, he saw her make another tour of the goldfields.

Burke was infatuated. She had auburn curls and a charm-

in their book *Will She Be Right?* They concluded that Australia may still be able to give the world a lead in one important respect. Both in its agriculture and mining, fewer and fewer people can produce more and more (hence a continuing drift to the cities); such industry as exists, because of imported computerised technology, requires fewer workers as well. Thus an increasing number of Australians are becoming available for tertiary services – and for leisure. A greater proportion than in any comparable country have surplus purchasing capacity, can afford to retire early, buy second homes and indulge their leisure interests. Australia therefore should have something to teach us about the shape of future life in a post-industrial, post-Christian society; in doing so, it will help to indicate what the West's new priorities and values will be.

Australia clearly tempts the sweeping judgement; as the only continental mainland peopled by a single nation, it attracts the large-scale generaliser. And inevitably, every microscope that is directed towards it will see only a small part of the whole, and then not always accurately. It has been wisely written about the various generalising books on Australia that they are 'expressions of the author's vision, of the imaginative effort he must make to create a representation of an exceedingly complex and hence ambiguous domain of existence. The reality of what goes on among the millions of people on the Australian continent is immensely different from the reality of ink on paper. To get from one to the other, a writer must select, compress, simplify, distort . . .'

Acknowledging these limitations, I can only hope that the following account has the merit of objectivity, combined with a friendly sympathy towards the country – if such virtues may be claimed by any Pom – and that a view from the train is often more informative than a series of conversations with leading intellectuals, plus a few impressionistic chapters on the bush. At least there is no spiritual journey going on at the same time to distract or distort: there are enough accounts by those Getting Away From It All and Seeking To Discover Themselves. I went to discover the spirit not of myself, but of Australia.

I

The North-West

Dawn points, and another day
Prepares for heat and silence. Out at sea the dawn
    wind
Wrinkles and slides. I am here
Or there, or elsewhere. In my beginning.
                (T. S. Eliot, 'East Coker')

Australia is the driest continent. In the north-west corner
of it nothing is abundant save spinifex, useless to man,
except that some Aborigines rub its spiked grasses together
and make a resin to bind their hunting weapons.

No tree grew and no bird flew. Nor was there any noise,
apart from the wind off the sea in the tufts of spinifex, and
the murmur of cicadas hiding amongst them. Even the flies
clung to my shirt quietly, waiting for the dawn.

Then a light shone from the hills, the oldest hills in
Australia, and strengthened as it approached. It shone from
a train, from the front of three diesel engines. Behind
them, silent too, were so many wagons – each filled with a
hundred tonnes of iron ore – that in terms of tonnage this
was the largest freight train running regularly anywhere in
the world.

These trains come down to the sea from a mountain
inland, and they bring the mountain with them. Mount
Tom Price is high-grade iron ore: machines and men eat
away at it as if levelling the pyramids. So rich is this region
of the Pilbara in its deposits of iron that it alone can supply
the world's needs at the present rate of consumption for
an estimated thousand years.

This train was pulling thirty, forty wagons of ore; eighty,
ninety, a hundred wagons, brakes shrieking as they de-

scended from the hills; one hundred and fifty, two hundred
. . . two hundred and ten wagons in all clanged past me on
their way to the port of Dampier a couple of miles down
the line, where ships waited to carry their load to the
steelworks of Japan. In Dampier the train, of more than
20,000 tonnes, halted, its wagons banging together like a
sonic boom, before silence returned to the wind and the
flies, the rising sun and the spinifex.

On the opposite side of the world, in a Somerset village,
the parish church of St Michael stands beside a manor
house in a country churchyard full of cedars, oaks and
beech trees. Inside, a bronze plaque hangs upon a cool
stone wall. It bears a handsome face surrounded by ringlets
and the inscription:

> To the memory of William Dampier
> Buccaneer, Explorer, Hydrographer
> and sometime Captain of the Ship Roebuck
> in the Royal Navy of King William the Third.
>
> Thrice he circumnavigated the Globe
> and first of all Englishmen
> explored and described the coast of Australia.
> An exact observer
> of all things in Earth, Sea and Air,
> he recorded the knowledge won by years of
> danger and hardship in Books of Voyages
> and a Discourse on Winds, Tides and Currents
> which Nelson bade his midshipmen to study,
> and Humboldt praised for scientific worth.
>
> Born at East Coker in 1651,
> He died in London in 1715,
> and lies buried in an unknown grave.

It is strange that James Cook should be widely considered
the discoverer of Australia. Dampier of East Coker pre-
ceded him there by almost a century, and even before
Dampier this north-west coast and the islands off 'New

Holland' were touched by Dutch ships, perhaps by Portuguese and Spanish ones too. Dampier arrived in 1688 as a member of the buccaneering crew of the *Signet*; in 1699 he returned here in the *Roebuck*, commissioned by William III to see more of *Terra Australis*. He explored the Dampier Archipelago, found it unattractively arid, collected plants for the Herbarium at Oxford and made observations on the wild life – which in his eyes included the Aborigines. He described them as 'the miserablest people in the world', and as such they became the model for Dean Swift's yahoos, when Gulliver travelled to the country of the Houyhnhms.

A train called the Spinifex Express once ran through the land of the Houyhnhms, though there is no sign of it on any map now. It started in Port Hedland, not far up the coast from Dampier, and operated as a narrow-gauge line until 1951. But long before then it had acquired the reputation of being a nightmare posting, dreaded by the railway men who were sent up from Perth by ship to do an unbroken three-year stint there. For they had gone and built the railway from Port Hedland to Marble Bar, and everyone in Australia knew that Marble Bar was the hottest place in the whole country. It's not simply that the mercury once climbed higher there than anywhere else: rather it's the continuousness of the heat that's the killer. The actual record was set on April 7 1924 when it was found that the shade temperature in Marble Bar had reached 100°F for the previous 160 days. But they'd known what the heat would be like when they decided on the railway, and it's still like that: daily, for six months every year, the small town is baked in its dish of volcanic, treeless hills.

But gold had been discovered in Marble Bar, and gold makes anything possible. It was the key to the development of the outback of Australia – gold followed by railways. So when the Premier of Western Australia, Hon. N. J. Moore, rose in the Legislative Council in Perth and moved the second reading of his railway Bill – 'which I feel sure if assented to by both Houses of Parliament will have a great bearing on the future prosperity of Western Australia, more particularly that district known to us as the

23

north-west' – it was overwhelmingly voted through and in 1909 construction began.

A causeway had first to be made from Port Hedland to the mainland, and this was laid over the top of mangrove saplings: they were thought to be a sturdy enough base for a train which never had to pull more than 250 tons and allowed itself eight hours for the 114-mile run. So they were. However, sandflies lurked in the mangrove and continued to live there and to fill the two passenger carriages (which were all that the line boasted) when they were left overnight in the sidings. And when they were disturbed for the once-a-week journey to Marble Bar they are said to have rivalled the heat in the discomfort they inflicted on unfortunate passengers.

But mostly it was the heat that won. Word got round and the contracting company began to find difficulty in getting enough labourers to finish the line. One man died of exhaustion: another fell off a motorised trolley and was a bloated carcass by the time he was discovered. Five more men were working on the track when they made a fire one evening to cook their meal, using readily available sleepers made of jarrah timber. Unfortunately they had already been treated with arsenic to deter the white ants . . . all five of the men were buried at the Twelve Mile mark outside Port Hedland. Eventually the private contractors had to hand the work over to the state government, and it was completed in 1912.

Laurie O'Byrne, a third-generation mix of Welsh and Irish, is one of the handful of survivors who worked on that railway. When I met him in the bar at Perth Station he had just made an emotional retirement after forty-five years on the state railways. For him Port Hedland was a place of sadness, not only because he had been caught up in a brawl when the line was closed down against local wishes – and he took out his teeth to show me the scar on his lip to prove it – but also because he had lost his first wife there. Nevertheless, he willingly recalled his working life, and the train which was so slow, and so friendly, that the guard would stop to boil a billy of tea for all its passengers and which came to be known as the friendliest train in Australia.

'I first went up there on December 27, 1948. There was three of us on the locomotives, and a station-master – Mr Harold Hearne – and his clerk and his guard. Besides being paymaster as well at Port Hedland, Mr Hearne used to control the whole lot and act as station-master at Marble Bar. A very fine man of his profession was Mr Hearne, my word he was.' At which O'Byrne, stocky and balding, raised a cold glass to drink his health.

'We ran the trains according to the state shipping, and as the ships came in on the tide and went out on the tide we weren't always so regular. We also brought in the water twice a week from Shaw River – beautiful fresh water – for the 800-odd people living in Port Hedland at that time. In the morning I'd take about forty-five minutes to get steam up. It would be a little 0–6–0 with a long funnel – she was a beauty–or the 2–6–0, which we called the Big One. I used to put a couple of large pieces of coal in by the door overnight, but you didn't tell 'em that because that was a "boiler unattended", which is not allowed. And then we'd be off about nine o'clock in the morning across the causeway.

'The sandflies? Goodness gracious me.' Mr O'Byrne paused to chuckle and wash away the memory. 'Yeah, we used to take the sandflies from the mangrove swamps across to Marble Bar, and they said, "Don't bring those bloody things over here!" But once across the causeway I've never seen such pretty country as up there in spring: Stuart's Desert Pea, miles and miles of it as far as the eye could see, bright red and pink and blue. But in summer it was all spinifex – not that it's bad food for sheep in winter-time, but in summer when it's dry you can always tell a sheep that's been trying to eat it by the needles sticking out of its gums.

'At times the track would warp but we'd follow it along. One day I spat on the line and it sizzled, that's God's honest truth. I'd keep my feet in a bucket of water, like the driver did and had to shovel four tons of coal each way – Newcastle coal. But I was a young man, I was strong, I was a tough little bugger! I wore a pair of shorts and a big hat, put a wet cloth round my neck and went as brown as a bloody berry.

'No, we didn't drink beer. We had two waterbags in the cab, and I had to drink so much water that I'd vomit it up to have some more. Then a native chap told me: he said get a little piece of cloth and put some salt in it, stick it under your tongue and suck on it all day. But I'd still break out in prickly heat – oh, you've no idea what a shocking thing that was. You lay awake at night and all of a sudden it'd come out in great big lumps on your arms.

'When we got to Marble Bar about four in the afternoon we used to have a shower in the railway barracks. We had our own shower there with a tank under the roof which kept the water cool, and we locked it up because all the locals wanted to use it when their water was too hot and stinking. Then we'd have our tea down at the pub, the Ironclad – it used to cost, in those days, I think it was six shillings – and they put on a beautiful meal, don't you worry about that. The outlying stations always had fresh meat to sell, you see. Then after a few more beers we'd walk down the creek to the barracks and shake out the bed rolls, as you never knew how many scorpions might have got into them since the previous week.

'Next morning we'd first make up our train – shunt everything around – then we'd have another shower and go back to the hotel for our breakfast. They'd cut us some beautiful crib to take back – sandwiches and that – and on the way home we'd shoot a few kangaroos, for stews. We bought this bloomin' shotgun and chased them along the track, then I'd go and hit 'em on the head with a bloody big poker. Of course we'd stop the train, why not? But we only did it for survival rations, you know. And wild turkeys too, "bustards" we called them: we cooked 'em back in Port Hedland – beautiful.'

O'Byrne finished his glass and 'shouted' another round. As condensation trickled down the outside of the fresh glasses, he went on to mention Bob Parollo who had the unique distinction of helping to lay the line back in 1912 and being the track-master when they pulled it up in 1951. The railways had honoured him by allowing him to keep that position until beyond the age of sixty-five. 'Old Bob had come over from Italy in the early days but he couldn't speak Italian – he had lost his mother tongue. He couldn't speak English either. He'd got a little local language of his own, and the only man who could understand him was our guard.

'Old Bob reckoned that line was his – he loved it, helped to lay it. Then one night we had heavy rains and the rivers flooded – one moment they can be dry and five minutes later they're sweeping down. And Bob came along to see where the train had to go along a creek bed, with an old pipe in his mouth, and he saw the water was only about eighteen inches deep, so he thought he'd go through it on his trike or trolley. But the rush of water had swept the line over about nine inches, which meant Bob and his trike went for a swim in the creek. He finished up a quarter of a mile down on the other side. But he was all right, just as he was the time he was knocked off his trike by a 'roo.

'It was called the friendliest train in Australia, the old Spinifex Express, but I don't know about that,' O'Byrne concluded. 'I was feeling grief when I was up there: I'd just lost my first wife in childbirth in Port Hedland, so I don't know what I really felt. But I'd certainly call it the loneliest.'

Today only the outdoor heat is the same in Marble Bar. Everything else has been modernised, a little suburbia has grown up, the trains and track have gone, and Laurie O'Byrne wouldn't recognise it. The majority of workers amongst its 500 people are employed in air-conditioned government departments like Community Welfare and Education, or by East Pilbara shire council. (East Pilbara shire, of which Marble Bar is the administrative seat, is two and a half times the size of the United Kingdom; it has 10,000 inhabitants.) Bungalows – 'transportable homes' – have been brought in by road, not train; they rest securely on a mortgage and concrete blocks. Pipes, wires and aerials bring in all amenities. Sprinklers twirl on the patch of lawn in front of every bungalow. The kids go biking in the hour before dusk, and no one has to suffer hardship any more.

Even the old Ironclad has air-conditioners and refrigerators to cool the beer, in place of hessian sacks sprayed with precious water. Pre-fabricated bedroom units have been added out the back, although they have not entirely replaced the old character: one evening, when cleaning my teeth at a wash-basin, not one but two frogs popped up the plughole to say good night. Outback towns like Marble Bar may still be 'rugged' in the eyes of those who live in the state capitals, but the people no longer have to be rugged to survive there. It's the same throughout the Pilbara. They may be pioneers, these men who explore the natural gas fields off the north-west coast or excavate Mount Tom Price or keep the ore trains running down to Dampier, but they all live in bungalows, shop with their wives in supermarkets and look ahead to their weekend barbecue.

It was an actual stockman from Marble Bar on whom Nevil Shute based part of his hero in *A Town Like Alice*: the local story is that this stockman was the one who had the bravado to steal the chickens from in front of Japanese officers. But that era, hardly more than a generation ago, seems to have gone. The improvising, daring, swearing, sweating, at times heroic Australian has become a grandfather or is dying out in these bungalows. His sons and grandsons are specialists, white-collar, car-owning, video-watching, eating and drinking as much or more, yet no longer called upon to burn off that energy except in raising children and planning for their better future.

There's a striking parallel here between Australia and Arabia. Both their peoples were originally hardened by the semi-desert; then nature changed from being hostile – it took their side, and its wealth from under the desert floor made their life easy. Now Australians, having fought their wars – against enemies abroad and nature at home – want to relax and enjoy themselves. It would be foolish, and unfair idealism, to expect them to do anything else.

However, surburban life was not what I sought, but rather 'the real Australia', which everyone talks about and few can precisely locate. So I took the train from Perth and started looking.

2

Perth to Adelaide

Damn Coolgardie! Damn the track!
Damn it there and damn it back!
Damn the country! Damn the weather!
Damn the goldfields altogether!

(Anon)

The Indian-Pacific could be another Orient Express, from a first sight of its passenger list. Down one column the names hint at diamonds, intrigue and dalliance on the journey to come: 'Lady Graves, Lady Bennett, Lady Malony . . .' Every carriage seems to be a *Burke's Peerage* in motion; no wonder Western Australia calls itself the State of Excitement. Anticipation waters at the mouth, the camels sniff the air and are ready to be gone! Then the eye catches a second column of names, each one paired off anticlimactically with its counterpart: 'Gent Graves, Gent Bennett, Gent Malony . . .'

Around ninety per cent of the clientele, at least on the Indian-Pacific I travelled on, was composed of grandparents returning to the eastern states, using to the maximum the free rail pass to which pensioners are entitled every year. When it pulled out at nine o'clock, Mendelssohn from Melbourne was being piped through the carriages. Not a tumultuous departure: young arms wave, some old eyes glisten. Passing through Perth's suburbia, past Pizza Huts and drive-ins, the train is pedestrian in its thirty mph beginnings. The conductor announces meal times over the intercom and that at Kalgoorlie next morning the train will stop long enough for passengers to make a tour of the town. The perms and their balding partners retire to bed in 'roomettes' and 'twinettes'. Solid and respectable. Mendelssohnian.

In the lounge bar some passengers stayed up for a drink, but not many princesses and their jewel-thief lovers. No one plays the famous piano, hallmark of the Indian-Pacific, in this television age. No longer are telegraphed dispatches of world news posted daily. One solitary man kept alive the tradition of the long-distance train: he was trying it on with a maiden aunt who had frozen, lace handkerchief to lips, over her nightcap Bailey's. He sat, lace-up shoes and hair equally black and sleek, perhaps a New Australian born in the eastern Mediterranean whose accent had been manicured for membership of the Melbourne Club. While the object of his intentions stole nervous glances at the escape route, he crossed his legs and expatiated on the trial then in progress of Pastor Michael and Lindy Chamberlain, whose baby had disappeared at Ayers Rock, devoured as they alleged by a dingo entering their tent: 'I would like to fly to Darwin to find out for myself all aspects of this case.' He lifted a languid paw: 'But I do not think the mother is a wicked woman – misguided, yes, but not wicked.'

The Indian-Pacific is sealed. Doors are not only shut but locked, the windows cannot open. The Lounge Lizard moved in on his prey: 'Tomorrow evening we will have half an hour while the train stops in the middle of the Nullarbor, at Cook – we can go for a walk then, together.'

She rose at that, and scuttled off to her roomette.

On June 13, 1893 Paddy Hannan was on the brink of immortality. He had come a long way to achieve it, from County Clare where he had been born in 1842. Since Clare was then one of the poorer counties in a famine-stricken Ireland Hannan had sailed for Melbourne at the age of twenty, inspired by stories of Ballarat gold. He spent his first four years in Australia mostly underground, not prospecting for gold by himself but working for wages: for already the initial stage of individuals fossicking on the surface with a shovel had mostly been overtaken by companies with the capital to employ labour, sink deep shafts and mine the reefs of gold-laden quartz far below.

But Paddy Hannan appears to have been a natural loner, one of those men who will spend months in the outback without talking to more than a dozen souls and who end up knowing by heart the couple of books which they take along in their swag for company. 'A rugged and unpretentious figure is Patrick Hannan,' says a contemporary description. 'He is undoubtedly a fine specimen of an Irishman, and combines in his person those splendid qualities of pluck and determination which have made so many Irishmen the pioneers and developers of so many lands of the new world.' He was also, and unusually, a temperate man by the standards of his native country and his day. Medium of height, quiet and equable, he followed the gold rushes as they came and went in New Zealand, Tasmania and Queensland, always slightly behind the vanguard but still making enough to pay his fare on towards the next illusory El Dorado. He did not pursue the rainbow's end out of a lust for riches, however; when Hannan sluiced the mixture of water, sand and crushed quartz around in his prospecting dish to let the gold dust settle at the bottom − or winnowed, if there were no water, by tossing the lot into the air so that everything but the gold (which is heaviest) blew away − he did not see in the gleaming specks left behind any visions of courtesans and luxury. His satisfactions, we gather, were more those to be found in the thrill of the chase.

By 1892 the hunt for gold was centred on Western Australia. Starting in Victoria, gold rushes had gone round the country in an anti-clockwise direction: from Queensland the prospectors had worked through the Northern Territory in the 1870s, round through the Kimberleys and the Pilbara of Western Australia (including Marble Bar) during the 1880s, and were now tempted by the potential of Coolgardie. A mine known as Bayley's Reward started a rush there in the winter of 1892; Hannan, who had been working to the south, joined in late and as usual found a little rather than a lot. But when summer started the diggers around Coolgardie had to abandon the gold for the even more precious commodity of water. Shortage of this had been the one great deterrent to prospectors eager to push ever further inland. In the area around Coolgardie, 390 miles east of Perth, sufficient rainwater collected in holes in the granite rock for natives to live on, but there was none to spare in summer for new arrivals. The last permanent water-hole was in Southern Cross, 250 miles east of Perth, which even today is the limit of man's cultivation of fields of grain. Beyond is desert, often full of trees, paradoxically green at times, but without water.

In the winter of 1893 prospectors returned to Coolgardie, and happily for them it was a wet year. In the cool of early June reports came in of a strike at Mount Youle to the north-east. In the stampede that followed Hannan was towards the rear, as he and a couple of mates had trouble in hiring horses – not surprisingly, since the price of a horse would jump tenfold in Coolgardie whenever the word went round that gold had been found in nearby hills. His mates were fellow Irishmen, Tom Flanagan and Dan Shea, and together they set out on June 7 upon horses that were elderly and poorly shod. They were getting on a bit themselves too, Paddy being the youngest of them and he at fifty no longer a broth of a boy. It took them three days to ride twenty-five miles to the north-east, where a shrub was growing called 'galgurli', an edible kind of native pear.

Who found what, exactly when and where has never been established. But it was beside a chain of mounds rather than hills; whether it was June 14 or 15 scarcely matters; and Hannan, not Flanagan or Shea, has always been given the credit since the other two were shoeing a horse at the time. But the discovery itself was beyond doubt: it lay there in small gullies, washed clear by the recent rain and alluring as only this one mineral has ever been. Gold is permanent both in its nature and attraction, except for Aborigines who see no use for it.

One of the three prospectors had to register this find in Coolgardie. As the youngest, Hannan was chosen to go, and being the man he was he took none of their water supply because he thought the claypans might hold enough for him; and when it rained again he even stopped, filled his bags and took them back to his mates. Not until the evening of June 17th did he reach Coolgardie to lodge his claim in the tent that served as the office of Warden Finnerty. Current laws of the state entitled him to a government reward of several hundred pounds for opening up an undeveloped area; and to twenty acres of ground surrounding the strike, provided it was more than twenty miles from any other gold mine, which in this case it marginally was. So the warden wrote out a reward claim in the name of Paddy Hannan, and posted it on the board outside his tent.

Frenzy broke loose as soon as Hanan's claim was seen. Exaggeration increased the size of his find one hundredfold; every man rushed off to find horses, stores, water, and at first light set off on the trail to Kalgoorlie. By the end of the week 2,000 men had departed from Coolgardie for Hannan's Rush, and at the start of it the town's entire population had only been 1,492. But while a few found the end of the rainbow the majority pursued it as vainly as ever. All Hannan and his friends had discovered was the alluvial gold that is washed to the surface, whereas the real worth was locked up in the deeper reefs or lodes of quartz, too far down for mere pick and shovel to reach.

Again it was a case of companies buying up the claims of individual prospectors and moving in – Australia can claim to be more egalitarian than most, but it has always had its moneyed élite. A South Australian syndicate bought up land a couple of miles to the south-east of Hannan's claim and there hit upon the Great Boulder mine, which forms a major part of the Golden Mile. By 1896 – in only two years – the Great Boulder had produced over a ton of gold at the current price of four pounds an ounce. By 1969, when the mine was shut down because the price of gold was too low to make further mining worthwhile, it alone had yielded six and a half million ounces. Other mines on the Golden Mile – the Boulder Perseverance, the Ivanhoe, the Golden Horseshoe – had each produced almost half as much. Kalgoorlie's Golden Mile was called the richest square mile of land on earth, and to date has yielded over 1,200 tonnes of gold.

Having been bought out at the going, niggardly rate, the prospectors took off into the bush again to continue searching, mainly to the north. Hannan himself wanted to escape the shenanigans and went to the coast for a holiday. He hadn't really struck it rich, merely paved the way for big business; and even if he had made a million he was the kind who might not have known what to do with it. He did not return to Kalgoorlie until 1897 when, once his grey beard and wiry frame had been spotted in the streets, he was begged to point out the precise spot where fame had come to him, and it was arranged for a tree to be planted there in commemoration. But – typical of Paddy – he wouldn't take the limelight and the mayor of Kalgoorlie's daughter had to plant it for him. He lived on in Victoria until 1925, by which time he had received all of two thousand nine hundred and twenty-five pounds as pension from the Western Australian government – this for the discoverer of the richest goldfields in the world, which were already worth one hundred million pounds to Australia by the time he died.

On November 15, 1925, eleven days after his death, one 'Dryblower' (E. G. Murphy) published a poetic obituary of Hannan:

> Roaring days have come and gone,
>   Claims must peter out;
> Younger men and younger ways
>   See we round about.
> Swagger clothes instead of swags,
>   No more tents and tramps,
> No more crashing choruses
>   In the mining camps;
> No more sing-song at the soaks;
>   No more golden dreams.
> *Tempus fugit*, someone says –
>   Dunno what it means;
> But it seems to suit the case
>   When you're out of teens . . . .
>
> Mates o' mine, O, mates o' mine,
>   Pals and pioneers!
> Let there be no sad repine,
>   Let there be no tears.

God has got the Golden Claim
All above the clay,
For Old Paddy Hannan,
Flanagan and Shea.

But not all private companies were successful at cashing
in on Hannan's discovery. In June 1894 the Golden Hole
was found, a deposit of quartz that after one rich haul lived
up only to the second half of its name. The Earl of Fingall,
however, happened to be in Coolgardie at that very moment
for the opening of its stock exchange, and his lordship was
on the look-out for investments in gold mining, as was
most of the City of London in the 1890s when other trade
was going through a world-wide slump. Fingall rushed off
to peer down the nearby mineshaft; history is remiss for
not recording whether he actually exclaimed, 'By Gad!' or
not, but he must have been agreeably surprised, for –
although he did not know a thing about geology – he told
the diggers who owned the hole that his London syndicate
would buy it from them for one hundred and eighty thousand pounds, an offer that was eagerly accepted. Fingall
doesn't appear to have known much about Australians
either, since he ordered the hole to be sealed and sailed to
London under the impression that some cement, a fence
and a guard would preserve his mine inviolate.

Back in London Fingall formed the Londonderry Gold
Mine Limited, with capital of 700,000 shares at one pound
each which were immediately bought up. The good lord
declared that 'it is most improbable that the rich quartz of
the "Londonderry Mine" (his name for the hole) can be
surpassed at the present time in the universe'. If the mine
went down a thousand feet, he continued, it would be
worth fifteen million pounds. As London became feverish,
Fingall, by now a national figure, returned to Australia
early in 1895 and descended again down the narrow shaft.
What he uttered this time also went unrecorded – perhaps
mercifully since, from Coolgardie post office, he had to
dispatch, on April 1 of all dates, an embarrassed telegram
to his board in London saying: 'Regret in the extreme have
to inform you that rich chutes of ore opened very bad

indeed stop Does not appear to be practically anything important left.'

As in most examples of boom-and-bust in the City of London between the South Sea Bubble and Poseidon, the only investors to be indignant were those who did not sell early and were left holding the shares when the music stopped. Fingall was never forced to do 'the decent thing' with a revolver; indeed, he persisted in floating gold-mining companies, as did so many other speculators that on average one new Western Australian company was floated every day in London for the next two years. If much of the money went in dividends to retired army officers in Surrey, a lot of capital nevertheless was invested in Western Australia, making life in Coolgardie and Kalgoorlie as intoxicating then as it must have been in California in '49.

People migrated into Western Australia, almost all of them men, in such numbers that the state's population rose from 28,000 in 1890 to 110,000 ten years later. Some arrived from overseas but the major source was Victoria, then Australia's most populous state, where the mines of Ballarat and Bendigo were losing their appeal. From Perth, Fremantle or the nearest railhead to Coolgardie they set off with swags on their back or their worldly goods on a wheelbarrow: a water-bag and flour for making 'damper', a hammer and prospector's dish, tea and canned beef (known as 'tinned dog'). A shade more affluent than these barrowmen were the swampers, who loaded their belongings on to a dray and followed on foot behind the horses. Some rode bicycles. Few were adequately prepared, with a dray or a camel team of their own to carry sufficient water and equipment. Too many set out with no knowledge of mining or local conditions or the granite outcrops where the few water-holes were located. For them it was a one-way journey: not a few bloated corpses were found, of men who had torn their clothes or scratched up the ground in the craziness of thirst.

Where only wilderness had existed at the start of 1892, by the turn of the century the third largest town in the state (after Perth and Fremantle) had sprung up – and to begin with only the prospect of gold in Coolgardie could have made tolerable the appalling lack of water. What there was had to be boiled and condensed, after being brought at great cost from brackish lakes. It was so precious that a gallon cost up to two shillings and sixpence, plus the Epsom Salts to make it drinkable, and while whisky bottles could be left on top of the hotel bars the water was kept underneath. Washing was never done in clean water: one man who wasted some on washing his feet was summarily put to death, even though as an Afghan camel-driver he had done it as part of his religious ablutions. Shacks or 'humpies' of hessian bags and tree trunks were the earliest housing in Coolgardie; fire frequently swept through them with nothing to quench it. No one bothered about sewers. Clothes were 'cleaned' by being buried in the sand for four days, hung on a line for three days, then worn for a week. Typhoid did not take long to appear.

The first prospectors who arrived in Coolgardie travelled under nicknames like Arizona Bill, Micky the Priest, Pigweed Harry, Old Alligator (since he was a snappy character) and Ragged Charlie. Acknowledging no one as master and perhaps with something to hide, they seldom disclosed their proper names to anyone; so that when the typhus or dysentery took them, they went into the graveyard unidentified by name or religion: indeed, half the first sixty burials in Coolgardie graveyard were of unnamed men. Frequently there was no time for anything more than a quick Lord's Prayer from the undertaker before the stranger was put in his shallow grave. Often a coffin would not be available, so packing cases were used instead. In the year when one half of Coolgardie was said to be busy burying the other half, some had makeshift coffins saying, 'Stow Away From Boilers'; and perhaps, after years in the furnace heat of Western Australia, they deserved to be thus spared in the afterlife, provided they had lived according to the miners' code of mateship, which meant sharing water even if it was the final drop they had.

It was the railway which brought relief. In 1896 a narrow (three-foot-six-inch) gauge track arrived in Coolgardie, to bring 15,000 gallons of water a day from the west, and reduce the price to fourpence a gallon. Life became almost

37

civilised. The horse drays no longer had to slog through the dust of summer or risk having their axles bogged in the mud of winter. Express mail from Coolgardie – of which there was plenty when speculators had to advise company boards in Perth and London – had cost five shillings per letter per day if delivered by cyclist, while a telegram from the post office had once cost a thousand pounds. The railway brought prices down to a level of sanity. Milk, for example, had cost a shilling a pint, if any were for sale, and an egg sixpence, the equivalent of a dollar today – inevitably, when everything brought up by horse or camel had cost one hundred and twenty pounds per ton.

Soon Coolgardie could boast one hospital, two stock exchanges, three breweries, four auditors, five timber merchants, six banks, seven newspapers (*The Coolgardie Miner* and *The Chronicle* were morning dailies, *The Golden Age* an afternoon daily, while four weeklies were published), eight auctioneers, nine tailors, ten restaurants and twenty-three hotels. Champagne was 'shouted' by the case, two and a half million litres of beer were consumed annually on the goldfields, and once a coffin was left outside an hotel all night after the mourners had stopped for just a quick one. This liquor went on fuelling gambling more than prostitution, so that betting on sport – especially on running and cycling – became the major entertainment in the absence of women.

The railway was a lifeline. It enabled men to drink uncontaminated water, and when they could afford a bath as well, women began to join them. Life was improved further in Coolgardie when in 1903 a water pipeline was opened. This marvel of engineering, unprecedented in the pre-oil pipeline age, took five and a half million gallons a day from a reservoir near Perth and pumped it not only 350 miles to the east but also up 1,200 feet in altitude. The scheme cost two and a half million pounds (too vast a sum for the state government to raise without overseas loans) and required 65,000 lengths of pipe. These pipes and the machinery for the eight pumping stations *en route* could be carried by train since the pipeline ran beside the track up to Kalgoorlie but during the construction everyone insisted on telling the head of the project, state engineer-in-chief Charles O'Connor (who had started his career on Irish railways), that he was crazy to try and make water flow uphill. Eventually he believed them and took his own life, a few months before his project was completed. Apart from the replacement of the original pipes with continuous-welded piping, the system works exactly the same and as well today, and can still be seen from the new standard-gauge train going from Perth to Kalgoorlie. There can be few better examples of Irish genius and madness being nearly the same.

This railway was a life-saver again in 1907 when a mining accident made front-page news for a fortnight around the English-speaking world, under the headline 'The Entombed Miner'. On March 19 torrential rain flooded a mine seven miles from Coolgardie at Bonnievale (now the last station before Kalgoorlie). Nineteen of the twenty miners down the shaft escaped that afternoon; the other was believed to have drowned. His name was Modesto Varischetti, an Italian who spoke little English, a widower of thirty-two with five children. Since he had twice before been trapped down a mine, Varischetti worked on the surface normally, but had volunteered to take the place of a fellow Italian miner who had to miss his afternoon shift. He had been working a thousand feet below when the rains started; when they stopped there was still a remote chance that he had been trapped in an air-pocket. Pumping machinery was brought in, the water in the flooded mine soon descended to the 900-foot level, and on the morning of the twenty-first tapping sounds were heard from below. But the rate of baling out the rest of the flood water was so slow that the local inspector of mines, by the unpoetic name of J. Crabb, reckoned it would be ten days before they could get to Varischetti, who was without light, food or even a source of air until a boring machine that had been near him at the time of flooding was switched on at the surface and compressed air forced through to him.

On the morning of the twenty-second Crabb telegraphed the Minister of Mines in Perth, asking for diving gear and

800 feet of hose to be dispatched as quickly as possible. In Perth a special train was prepared, comprising one coach, a brake van and a coal truck to give stability: for the train was aiming to beat the regular express's time of thirteen hours eight minutes. So fast did the rescue train go, after leaving Perth to cheering crowds, that it averaged over thirty mph on pioneer track in spite of two changes of crew, and finally steamed into Coolgardie at four a.m. on March 23 after a run of eleven hours and forty-four minutes. It was a record run; and even today the Prospector, on new standardised track, takes a good seven and a half hours to reach Kalgoorlie.

As soon as the diving equipment had been conveyed to Bonnievale an experienced diver called Hughes – day after day the papers never gave him a Christian name, although he was hero of the hour – went down the shaft to the cross-cut or horizontal tunnel at the clear 900-foot level. From there he dived down to the 1,000-foot tunnel along which the Italian was trapped. Although he could not find Varischetti, Hughes located the compressed-air pipe leading to the boring machine and when he tugged at it he felt a tug in reply. Later that same day Hughes dived again, to emerge through the flood water into the air-pocket where his lamp spot-lit the entombed miner. Encased himself in a full diving suit Hughes could not speak to him, but he left food for the incredulous Varischetti, who clearly had not seen diving gear before.

Pumping continued for the next five days as Hughes brought in daily supplies. Given pen and paper to while away his period of entombment the Italian wrote in his messages that he had given up hope. He bade an emotional farewell to his brothers and five *bambini*, but was sufficiently Italian to add that he thought the food which Hughes brought him was highly satisfactory. Finally, on March 28, nine days after it had gushed in, the water had descended far enough for Varischetti to be led along the 1,000-foot cross-cut, up to the 900-foot level, and thence to be lifted in a skip to the surface. The assembled crowd, having been instructed not to startle him, could not forbear to cheer, and it was a remarkable rescue, as were so many around the country's mines; but typical, too, of Australian improvisation, determination and heroism.

But even in 1907 Coolgardie was going into decline. The gold in surrounding outcrops was superficial, as Fingall was not alone in discovering; the deep-lying ores were to be found in the Kalgoorlie area. So the centre of the goldfields was shifted to Hannan's (as Kalgoorlie was popularly known) and Coolgardie became a ghost town. Many such are dotted around Western Australia – but little evidence of any of them remains, since their corrugated iron has been removed for building elsewhere, their wood has been stripped for fencing and the bush has taken back what had been temporarily usurped.

Kalgoorlie, however, lives on to prosper, the 30,000 population of its heyday shrunk no further than 20,000. Where there were eight breweries there is now only one, but Hannan's can cater for every local demand. Kalgoorlie's vital boost came in the 1970s when the gold price was no longer pegged at thirty-five dollars an ounce, so that it became worthwhile to re-open old mines and re-process old slag; before then it had become uneconomical to do much more than pick up nuggets. Nickel enjoyed a boom as well, after being found in the goldfields about 1900 and ignored until a world nickel shortage in the sixties. Australia's first nickel mine was then opened just outside Kalgoorlie, becoming the world's second commercial smelter.

Some of these sights can be seen by the rail traveller during the half-hour stop which the Indian-Pacific allows; also the place where Paddy Hannan said the commemorative tree should be planted. Close by it is the British Arms, which used to be – a curious boast – the narrowest hotel in the country and which, characteristically British in some Australian eyes, also owned the narrowest bar room, six measly feet across. One old gold mine is kept open for the tourist trade, and the guide explains that Kalgoorlie mines are shallow, not one of them so much as 5,000 feet, which is a quarter of the depth of some South African mines. And he'll give you the propaganda, which sounds a bit like some old Paddy Hannan blarney, that there is still far more gold

41

beneath the Golden Mile than has ever been brought to the surface.

Something else glisters temptingly in Kalgoorlie, and it is certainly not gold. Hay Street near the station is said to be the only red-light district officially allowed in Australia, and its two rows of corrugated-iron huts still stand, looking even more like outdoor lavatories than most one-storey buildings in Kalgoorlie. Unnatural blondes shine in the light of doorways, sitting in their coops, well siliconed like chickens, but not moving a muscle so as not to risk soliciting a patrolling policeman. In fact, however, prostitution is permitted to continue openly, as a social safety-valve since the male-female ratio is nearly as lop-sided as it ever was on the goldfields; and Madame is such a pillar of local society that her annual garden party is said to be a must for aspiring politicians.

As in hospital, meals come early on the Indian-Pacific – first sitting for dinner in the orange dining-car at five-thirty. Breakfast was so early that the sunlight was still filtering sideways through the bush, making it into dark-green cauliflower against a background of reddening earth. Mallee and mulga are the most common flora to the east of Kalgoorlie: mulga a wattle up to fifteen feet high, mallee of similar height, the name for a number of eucalypts with a cluster of stems rising from the ground. Few trees are higher because massive commercial deforestation by the 1920s gave the land a crewcut from which it has not yet recovered. The timber was felled for firewood to power the water-condensers and ore-crushing batteries, for fencing and propping up shafts and tunnels in the mines. The railways had a hand also in the destruction. Numerous narrow-gauge 'wood lines' were built to help fell these forests, starting in 1871 with the first railway in Western Australia, from Busselton south of Fremantle.

Breakfast was vast as well as early: an Australian train marches on its stomach. After cereals, juice and toast I vainly attempted eggs and bacon. The grandmother alongside me waded into sausages, mashed potato, onions and gravy; there were also lamb chops, or the inevitable steak

and eggs, *the* dish of old White Australia. One of the
most notable benefits of post-war immigration is that the
newcomers have brought their national cuisines with them.
There wasn't much variety in the old bush diet of steak
and eggs for breakfast, steak and eggs for midday tucker,
steak and eggs for tea. I found the ultimate bush menu
in the Refreshment Rooms at Hughenden. Chalked on a
blackboard it read:

5.30–6.45 Monday–Saturday
Rump Steak $4
T-bone Steak $4

Besides, steaks in Australia are often too well cooked,
while an egg is like John Aubrey's hope – it makes a good
breakfast but a poor supper.

One hundred and sixty-seven miles to the east of Kalgoorlie the scenery changes abruptly. As granite gives way
to the limestone of the Nullarbor Plain, eucalypts cease;
bluebush and saltbush take over, plants which can survive
merely by drinking dew. Earth becomes sandier and stonier,
the stones scattered about as on a beach at low tide, which
in a way is what it is – the sea having gone out millions of
years before. Every hour or so along the way the stones
have been gathered into a couple of cottages for the fettlers
who tended the old track, while every quarter of an hour
a crow or eagle may appear, or a nest placed atop an
abandoned bore-hole in the utter absence of trees. That the
train's trundling speed is forty mph is a meaningless piece
of information in this emptiness; relative progress is better
measured in terms of four crows per hour, or three rabbits,
or a couple of kangaroos bounding along the boundary
fence. And once a day the Indian-Pacific or Trans-
Australian passes in the opposite direction, the trains cross
slowly, one in a siding, and you see a startled passenger
lying in bed quickly pull the blind down.

If the art of living is to appreciate the subtle variations
in daily routine, the Nullarbor must be the place to practise.
An Indian-Pacific diary resembles that of Mark Twain's on
board ship: 'Got up, washed, went to bed', and for the

next day ditto. The options here are eat, sleep, read, or look out of the window; or look out of the window, read, eat and sleep. Even Mendelssohn can't be picked up any more as he is too far from the aerial on the carriage roof. Perhaps the most satisfying pastime is to contemplate the plain from the fold-up lavatory built into your roomette: pissing *en passant*, while the unspoilt earth goes by. From that vantage-point you can grasp immediately what the whole medieval world failed to understand: the curve of the horizon tells you unmistakably that the Earth isn't flat.

The Long Straight begins, 297 miles of it, still the longest section of straight track anywhere. Halfway along it is a board proclaiming 'Farewell to Western Australia'. Not long after, towards sunset of the second day, occurs the significant event of passing through Hughes, one of the largest fettler communities on the Nullarbor: a veritable city of the plain, it comprises five bungalows and some scrapped cars. Reid, Deakin, Hughes, Cook, Fisher – the names for these sidings or groups of cottages are derived from former Australian prime ministers, since there were no native names for these places in the middle of nowhere. Although it was within the province of the Mirning tribe, they rarely went on to the plain because they knew the serpent Jeedara would drag the unwary underground and into the Great Australian Bight almost a hundred miles away. Their myth had a geological rationale: there are limestone caves down which the unwary can disappear – blow-holes, some sucking in air, others exhaling, and inhabited by dingoes.

After a while it seems unjust that all these sidings across the Nullarbor should have been named in memory of the prime ministers or governors-general who came to inspect the line – and to be photographed inspecting it – during its construction between 1913 and 1917, and not a single one of them after a member of the navvy gangs who sweated along its length. They moved five million cubic yards of rock and earth between Kalgoorlie and Port Pirie; in all those 1,052 miles, the distance between London and Algiers or Latvia, there was not one river or stream to sustain them. The 3,500 men on the line had to make do with

44

shooting wild turkeys and with the rations brought along on the 'Tea and Sugar' supply train – which still runs weekly – washed down with sly-grog, which they called bluebush juice, and made of overproof whisky, meths, boot polish and water, all for fifteen shillings a bottle. Once a week, on Sunday, they were given a small kerosene can of water in which to have a bath; and better still, once a week they had pay-day, after which they played dice and the coin-tossing game of two-up until all their money had changed hands, the winners going off to Port Pirie or Adelaide to blow the lot, until they too were broke and had to return to the railway for work.

It was said on Federation day in 1901 that Western Australia had only agreed to join on the condition that a railway line would be built as a tangible link between east and west. But the state premier Sir John Forrest would have had to join on any terms, after Kalgoorlie's miners had threatened to secede from Perth otherwise and take their gold with them. Surveying began in 1908; 250 camels were employed, along with 500 horses in spite of their mutual antipathy, plus a tracklayer operating from each end. That the route went inland, rather than along the coast of the Bight where the modern road goes, was due to consider-ations of war not economy: like Canberra, the line would be safe inland fom shelling by enemy ships. And when the 2,500,000th sleeper had been laid and the two ends linked in 1917, John Forrest received a peerage – Baron Forrest of Bunbury, the first Australian-born peer – while the navvies went on the dole when depression followed war.

On the evening of the second day out from Perth the Indian-Pacific neared Cook in the middle of the Nullarbor. Lounge Lizard shifted restlessly in his seat, remembering his promise to the maiden aunt. As the sun set directly behind the train the saltbushes went from silver to grey, the sky from red to brilliant orange – as orange as the fittings and curtains in the dining-car. It was that lurid.

Annually 100,000 people stop in Cook, if there isn't a strike on. That makes the place sound like a bustling metropolis, but not one of those passengers stops longer than half an hour, either in the evening on the train heading east or in the early morning *en route* to Perth. Certainly Lounge Lizard (strolling alone, I noticed) did not linger. Furthermore, I was told that the only person to have stayed longer had been a stowaway discovered on board some years before, who would have passed the night in one of Cook's two lock-up cells before being shipped back again, were it not for the fact that the stowaway was a she and the lock-ups therefore thought unsuitable. I broke the rule, however, and stayed.

Cook consists of a street. On one side are the track and station, on the other a line of bungalows. A hundred and one people live there, over ninety of them employed by Australian National Railways; the others are a couple of schoolteachers, a nurse and their children. At the eastern end of 'town', towards Adelaide, are the two lock-ups. They are of corrugated iron, seven feet by seven feet: one is furnished with some planks to form a bed, the second is more primitive. The absence of graffiti substantiates the claim that they are used no more than twice or thrice a decade, but as the nearest policeman lives eight hours down the line in Tarcoola the drunk-and-disorderly have a chance to sober up before authority arrives by train.

Cook's most striking characteristic is that generosity in material things so common in Australia. 'A bed for the night? No worries,' said the assistant station-master. How about a beer, come and join the barbecue tonight, have a steak – the rough-diamond qualities of Aussie mateship. Over the beer and barbie, conversation focused, perhaps inevitably, on the imbalance between men and women which existed in Australia till after the Second World War and remains a feature of the outback. There can't be many places where there isn't an unmarried woman for 700 miles, but I was assured that this is the situation between Tarcoola and Kalgoorlie's red-light district. 'What do I do about it?' asked a bare-chested, tattooed thirty-year-old who was cooking the steaks. 'I just don't think about it, that's all. You can either go to Kal [on one of the six free rail passes which railway employees receive in Cook per year], have a quick screw and get thrown out, or you can go on the piss here every evening. And when you wake up in the mornings you go on the piss, and at weekends you spend all day on the piss. What else do you expect me to do?'

There is no television in Cook, and no commercial radio. It doesn't have many air-conditioners either, about one per bungalow, and they cannot cope with mid-summer. The place might well have acquired its name from the fact that you can fry an egg on the line on many days of the year. I was told that in January the thermometer hits 50°C in the shade, of which there is not an abundance. 'You get used to it,' said the cheerful assistant station-master, who had emigrated from Featherstone in Yorkshire. Birds drop from the sky, kangaroos and dingoes break into the tiny gardens to find food, section cars have to go ahead of the trains to make sure the track hasn't warped too badly. But you get used to it.

The most determined resident in Cook had stuck it for fourteen years. Although the railway workers' average stay was about five, most of them admitted they didn't mind being posted to Cook because of the opportunities for extra shiftwork, and younger lads even volunteer for a posting there to get quicker promotion. However, ANR prefer men with families for these outposts: married men drink but single ones drink more. Fights break out in fettler communities of two or three households even, with broken bottles used to create an impression on former friends.

This business keeps the hospital going at the western end of 'town'. Built by the Bush Church Aid Society in 1937, it used to deal with every case on its own and run an operating theatre, but now the Flying Doctor lands on the dirt airstrip outside and removes patients to Port Augusta, even pregnant women six weeks before they are due. The time of improvisation in intolerable heat or howling winds has gone – now, according to the sister in charge, it's cuts, dehydration, viruses and loneliness that have to be dealt with, and work is often slack. Hence the slogan she took me outside to point out, painted on a water-tank: 'If youre [sic] crook [sick] come to Cook.' She showed me the airstrip as well, and the primary school, and her garden walled with old sleepers and her hollyhocks standing against them, without once referring to the desert that dominated the entire view. To her there was nothing beyond the edge of human settlement, nothing worth mentioning, nothing but Nullarbor.

She made me wonder – while the train next evening took half an hour to arrive after the first glimpse of its light – why the white man continues to burden himself with this railway. All the freight which is carried across the Nullarbor in three or four trains a day and which keeps the line going financially could just as well be transported by ship, the passengers by plane. Recently some of the sidings have been closed down – Fisher, Deakin, O'Malley – but so long as this line lasts there will have to be outposts of men to maintain it and run the repeater stations, even when continuously welded rails have been laid on top of concrete sleepers.

By dawn next morning the mud flats of Lake Hart shone to the north of the track. Like most Australian lakes, it might as well have been named Lake Disappointment. An hour later appeared the first habitations for a thousand miles that were not connected with the railway: the complex of Woomera a few miles to the north, fed by a branch line.

Port Pirie was once the station where three gauges ran side by side down the main street, but passengers can nowadays ride on standard track the whole way to Sydney or Adelaide. I changed for the Adelaide train and passed through scenery as Mediterranean as any in Australia, created by Italians and Germans who came to these hinterland hills of South Australia and reproduced their farms and vineyards and orchards after the image of those at home. But drought had turned their green to yellow. Wheat that could not survive the driest period since the turn of the century had been ploughed back as stubble, and the land was like biblical Egypt condemned to seven lean years. Then to Adelaide, laid out primly and properly in grid pattern by Colonel Light in 1838: the most gracious of Australian cities.

3
Adelaide to Alice Springs

'Alice is a bonza place, oh my word. A girl's got everything in Alice.'

(Joe Harman in *A Town Like Alice*)

In the back streets of central Adelaide – beside the small
factory owned by Total Business Equipment, across the road
from the Duke of Brunswick, whose patrons are not under-
dressed if they enter in vest and shorts, and no more than a
couple of hundred yards from the TAB betting shop – four
slim white-washed towers loom above the telephone wires.
These are the minarets of the oldest mosque in Australia;
and this mosque is the starting-point of the story behind
Australia's most famous train, the Ghan.

I had been to Adelaide half a dozen times before coming
across this mosque. Islam tends to be inconspicuous – even
a secret society at times – in Australia, as in most Christian
countries. I would never have guessed that Australia has as
many as 200,000 Muslims, but that is the estimate of the
effective head of the country's Islamic community, the
Adelaide Imam, Imam Skaka.

A Yugoslav, like most Australian Muslims, Imam Skaka
has become absorbed into his adopted country's way of
life: he was wearing a watch he had recently received as a
retirement present from his mates, after twenty-five years
in a light engineering factory. But the first Muslims in
Australia were not inconspicuous: when they started coming to this mosque towards the end of the nineteenth
century they wore strange-looking bloomers and turbans.

One such Muslim was named Seed (an honorary title like
'sir') Sedeeq, who styled himself a camel-driver from Baluchis-
tan. While staying at this mosque before venturing into the
interior of South Australia to set up his trade, Sedeeq took a

49

fancy to a sixteen-year-old Scottish girl who worked on the premises, washing the clothes of other camel-driving Muslims who passed through Adelaide. She was pretty, and since there was not a single available woman of his own faith and nationality in Australia he proposed marrige to her. He already had a wife in Karachi and several children, but the Prophet himself – may Allah bless him and give him peace! – had taken four wives to his marriage bed, and how could an honest camel-driver be expected to live for years in a foreign land without the comfort of a spouse? In any event, she accepted him. So this Baluchi Muslim married a Presbyterian lass half his age, and set off into the interior to establish his camel business.

The first half a dozen camels to go to Australia had been transported there in 1854, but five died and the other fatally bit its owner, as even the best-behaved bull is liable to do in the mating season. The second consignment was for the Burke and Wills expedition in 1860, when twenty-four camels were brought from Karachi to assist in their transcontinental crossing, though not the least of the curiosities about their expedition was that they did not always ride their camels but chose to walk alongside them instead. These ships of the Sind and Gobi were soon found to be excellently suited to the Australian interior, however, and in 1867 twelve Afghan cameleers were signed on four- or five-year contracts and brought to South Australia with 123 dromedaries to form, after a lengthy quarantine period, the first camel-breeding station.

The explorer Ernest Giles, in particular, gave them the best of references after twice crossing Western Australia with their help:

> I could not sufficiently admire and praise the wonderful powers of these extraordinary and, to me, entirely new animals. The country we had traversed was a most frightful desert, yet day after day our noble camels kept moving slowly but surely on, with undiminished powers, having carried water for their unfortunate companions, the horses, and seeing them drop one by one exhausted and dying of thirst: still they marched contentedly on,

carrying us by turns, and all the remaining gear of the dead horses, and finally brought us to water.

These camels in South Australia carried copper at first from the Flinders Ranges down to Port Augusta, competing successfully with bullocks and some traction engines shipped from England which could not stand the heat. But their big break came when contracts were tendered for transporting poles and wires for the Overland Telegraph. In 1870 the British Australia Telegraph Company proposed to lay an underwater cable from Java to Port Darwin, just as the *Great Eastern* had recently done across the Atlantic. Since this telegraph was joined from Java through India to London it was going to bring more than a little prestige to the first Australian state to be on the receiving end of it and thus in direct contact with 'home'.

By this time Queensland already had a telegraph line running from Normanton near the Gulf of Carpentaria to Brisbane, and thence to the other eastern states: a relatively short extension therefore would link the whole system to Darwin and through Java to London. But so intense was state rivalry that South Australia would not countenance anything of the sort: Port Darwin was in the Northern Territory, the Territory then was under Adelaide's jurisdiction, and it was decided that Queensland should be kept out. Instead South Australia announced that it would construct a line from Darwin over almost 2,000 miles of unexplored desert to Adelaide, just so that it could have the honour of being the first to receive dispatches from London.

By 1872 the Overland Telegraph had been constructed, thanks in no small part to the Afghan cameleers, and as there were some surveyors left who had not perished of thirst it seemed only logical to add a railway beside the telegraph line. It would be a government project, unlike most contemporary railways in other countries, because prestige and the wish to open up land on either side of the line were more important considerations than commercial profit. Thus the Governor of South Australia, Sir William Jervois, turned the first sod in 1878 and wrote soon afterwards that Port Augusta would be 'the Southern terminus of a Transcontinental Railway, about 1,800 miles in length, which will ultimately be carried through the Province of South Australia to Port Darwin'. Today, over a century later, Jervois's vision has yet to be realised.

In its initial stages north of Port Augusta the railway followed the route that had been used by Aborigines for their long-distance trade in ochre which was required for ritual ceremony. By 1882 the railhead was at Government Gums, a name so lovely and euphonious that they went and changed it to Farina: the expansionist businessmen of Adelaide were hoping this region would become the granary of Australia and that Farina would be the centre of this 'flour power'. The trains used to potter up there on narrow-gauge track from Adelaide at twelve mph, prompting Mark Twain to suggest that the cow-catcher might as well be placed at the back. Nevertheless the railway was by far the most convenient form of transport into the interior, and already the longest in any state. In 1884 it was extended north to Hergott Springs (named after a German immigrant), to meet cattle driven down the Birdsville Track from Queensland and to freight them south to provide Adelaide with much of its beef. Even though the trucks were so poorly designed that cattle had to stick their heads over the side and sometimes had their horns broken off, the cattle men found the train ride still preferable to the long overland trek to Adelaide, at the end of which their stock might be so emaciated as to be unmarketable.

In this very outback town of Hergott Springs Sedeeq arrived with his Scottish wife and dreams of dromedaries. Although the line had then been extended onto Oodnadatta, Hergott Springs was the gateway not only for the Birdsville Track but also for Mount Hopeless, Innamincka and Nappa Merrie to the north-east. Many other Muslims had congregated too, not only Baluchis like himself. Unfortunately, no government records were ever kept of the origins of these cameleers when they immigrated, but from the list of donors to a mosque in Perth – where their tribal names are given in full – Imam Skaka has deduced that they hailed from a wider region than Afghanistan alone. There were men from north-west India – Sind, the Punjab and Rajputana – as well as Pushto-speaking Pathans from Afghanistan (numerically the largest section amongst these cameleers who had taken ship to Australia). Everyone else made fun of – but respected – these Pathans, ferociously proud and independent and not altogether scrupulous. 'Who's the only virgin on the North-West Frontier?' goes the stock joke. 'A goat that can run faster than a Pathan.' Or there's the saying: a woman for duty, a boy for pleasure, and a goat for pure delight.

But all the Muslims in Hergott Springs lived together, whatever their origin, under the label of 'Afghans', and stayed on the western side of the railway track. The 'whites' meanwhile – many no lighter-coloured than they – kept to the eastern side. Strings of camels, forty-five to fifty in a string, would stir up the dust in the main street of Ghan Town on their return from a three-month trek to Queensland, off to have the sores on their backs tarred or greased with kerosene, bellowing for a drink at the bore-holes, and commanded by cries of 'Hoosh! Hooshta!' Sedeeq built himself a house with a tin roof and three pepper trees in front, with a compound where the seven 'blackfellas' he employed would chew their tobacco wages and the young camels kept there would sidle up to the kitchen windows for a *chapatti*. The Afghans were fond of their camels: they were natives of the same home-land, together in a new country.

They built a shed for a mosque in Hergott Springs – or Marree as it was called after German names became un-popular during the First World War. They also cultivated a grove of date-palms, though the palms had to be polli-nated by hand unlike those at home. They had three shops of their own, selling general goods and the ritually slaugh-tered meat of young camels and goats, and a dance hall where their celebrations were held. They shared the school on the other side of the track, but it was about all they did share with the whites who called the Afghans 'dark clouds' – unless they wanted to do business with them. The actual dark clouds were those which built up to the north of Marree once or twice a week in summer and sent everyone rushing home to fasten their windows, but which still crept in to leave inches of dust over everything.

53

Seed Sedeeq built up his camel-carrying concern both in Marree, where he owned 350 camels, and in Farina. He did an increasing amount of work for Sir Sidney Kidman, 'the Cattle King', who made a million in the outback before the First World War, having left his Adelaide home at the age of thirteen on a one-eyed horse called Cyclops, with five shillings in his pocket; Kidman eventually owned more land than anyone else in the British Empire. Camels could go anywhere in the semi-desert, and did go as far south as Victoria and as far north as Newcastle Waters where Gastrolobium grew, a plant poisonous for camels. But Sedeeq specialised in the Birdsville Track, bringing wool down it and carrying up flour, tea, sugar, sardines, rice and even beer, although it was against his religion to touch the drink. But no pig meat: by Allah, he drew the line at pork or ham or bacon!

Yet Sedeeq was not the most famous of Afghan camel-eers; that had to be Abdul-Walid from Quetta who established the Bourke Carrying Company. He would contact his agents in Peshawar and Bikaner and have them bring camels to Karachi where he would meet them and conduct them to Australia – 750 camels at forty pounds a head in one consignment of 1892. He also brought out sixty camel-drivers, but they at least – even though some were wild Pathans – did not have to go through the ninety-day quarantine period.

During the late 1920s the Central Australian Railway was extended on from Oodnadatta to Alice Springs, and camels were no less essential then than they had been in the original construction. Sedeeq's camels could carry four sleepers on each flank and a rail laid across the top. They also carried miles and miles of rabbit- and dingo-proof fencing around the interior – reliably and fairly honestly too, though evil rumours were circulated by white camel-eers who liked to be paid four pounds a week compared with the Afghans' three pounds a *month* and were thus in lesser demand: rumours that Afghans were unclean and allowed their mangy camels to pollute the drinking water at bore-holes. Unclean? Afghans stopped to wash five times a day when they judged by the sun it was time to pray.

These tales were most likely a product of that resentment shown towards many a hard-working minority.

By his Scottish wife Sedeeq had three children. She was expecting a fourth when she fell down the cellar steps of her house in Marree. Because there was no doctor she was taken to the station and loaded into the guard's van of the weekly goods to Port Augusta, but she died during the journey. Later one of her sons drowned in Cooper's Creek on a trek to Queensland. In 1933 Sedeeq himself died, when the end was in sight for his camels. They could co-exist with a railway – maintaining the track, carrying mail and goods where the trains could not go – but they could not compete with the car and lorry. Marree means 'the place of many possums'; it also became the place of many slaughtered camels during the thirties when hundreds were taken out to the common, shot and left for the crows and dingoes. However, enough escaped from the various Ghan Towns of Australia for an estimated 15,000 to be roaming round the bush nowadays, their numbers growing.

Sedeeq's fellow Afghan cameleers were dying out as well, drifting to the cities to become street hawkers or else retiring. Their sons – by Australian wives, as they could never bring their own women with them – tended to join fettlers' gangs, their daughters to take up work in the railways as office workers or carriage cleaners. They became integrated, followed their mothers' Christianity if any religion, became Australian citizens (unlike their fathers, who were never granted naturalisation), and grew indistinguishable from white Australians. There may be several dozen Mahomets in the slender volume that is the Alice Springs telephone directory, but the only sign of their Afghan origin is the name.

This tale of Seed Sedeeq was told me by his daughter Allema. Now in her seventies, she lives on her own in a fine stone bungalow in a pleasant part of Adelaide, widowed, curly-haired, one-eyed – there having been no doctor in Marree to cure a childhood eye infection – and one of the few surviving offspring of the original Afghan immigrants. She told me she was the last who knew how to make the bloomer trousers for their marriages and dances, while sitting at her kitchen table, the blinds down to protect her good eye from the midday light, and rummaging through cupboard drawers for mementoes from her extraordinary past. She produced a newspaper cutting, dated 'Alice Springs, April 15, 1955':

One of the last of the original Central Australian camel drivers who freighted stores on teams of up to 80 beasts on long hauls from Marree to Alice Springs, died in Alice Springs Hospital today.

He was an Afghan, Abdul Mageed – everyone called him Mudgee – and his age was estimated at between 86 and 93.

'Mudgee' started operating camel trains in Western Australia in the early '90s, later moved to Tarcoola and then to Marree and Alice Springs.

He was a familiar figure about the town in moleskin trousers, black shirt and white turban. Bent almost double, his huge knotted hands used to grasp a barrow at the Commonwealth Railways goodsheds as he trundled from railvan to motortruck the wares that 30 years previously he had loaded on his camel team at Oodnadatta to bring to Alice the hard way.

He seldom looked at you, and when he did it was a sidelong glance from piercing eyes set above a hawklike nose. When young and strong he must have been an enormously tall man.

He must have been well over 80 when he was forcibly 'retired' from the railways here, but he still claimed in an exasperated 'pidgin' of his own, 'Blooty fellas hall h'rong – me bin onlee sikistee!'

Mudgee built himself a fine house in Alice Springs, and was reputed to have made a fortune from his cameleering days (estimated at £10,000) – but he didn't much like living in it and preferred the old humpy at the back, where he would dispense tea, lollywater and biscuits to anyone who cared to take it with him.

His only heirs live in a remote village in Pakistan.

'Lived at the old humpy out the back? He did too.'

Allema nodded. She was getting tired; the cockatoo on her verandah was asleep. As I rose to go she wanted to press five dollars on me from her barely adequate pension as a good luck present – Middle Eastern generosity wedded to Australian hospitality.

She had a walled garden which 'they' – the developers – were trying to buy off her along with the house, and they had dangled large sums in front of her to get it. She had refused. The concrete apartment units next door waited behind her trees and walls. 'Well, they're not going to have this place until I'm dead,' she said, proud, defiant, individual.

As Australia does not have an overwhelming interest in its past I think it's appropriate that the memory of these Afghan pioneers should have been perpetuated in the name of the train from Adelaide to Alice Springs, the Ghan. Exactly when the name stuck – whether it originated in the anecdote about an Afghan passenger stopping to pray beside the track at Oodnadatta in 1923, or in the fact that the construction trains going up to William Creek in the 1880s were half full of Afghans – can never be established and it hardly matters. It is 'the Ghan' and always will be, even the new standard-gauge version of it which has been running since 1980 via Tarcoola.

Perhaps inevitably, the new Ghan is to the old Ghan what the New English Bible is to the King James: modernised but lacking in mystery. It wasn't so much the drifting sand which made a journey on the old Ghan eventful, or the bushfires, or the occasional derailment, or the wild camels that had to be shunted off the line, or the plagues of grasshoppers and ants which at times swarmed so thickly that the rails were too slippery to grip. 'It was the clouds you had to watch out for,' a former driver told me, 'you always had to keep an ear and eye out for them.' The old Ghan ran along some creek beds that drained into Lake Eyre, and over flimsy bridges spanning others, and when the rain began torrential flashfloods would come down so suddenly that there might be no chance to avoid the on-coming rush. The best a driver could do was wait on higher ground till the flood subsided. Thus the Ghan was often delayed a week, sometimes for several weeks, once for three months; 200 passengers had to be air-lifted from the carriage roofs by helicopter in 1963; but few passengers complained, for none of them expected the old Ghan to keep to its schedule on worn-out narrow-gauge track.

The new Ghan is efficient and regular, as efficient and regular as it is unexciting. Not only in the matter of gauge has the route been standardised: it is now like a modern train journey anywhere else in sealed, air-conditioned carriages, having no more contact with the landscape it passes through than if the countryside were a cinema screen outside the window. You leave Adelaide in the morning, set off from Port Pirie in the afternoon and wake up next morning not far out of Alice Springs. Perhaps the surprising and wonderful thing is that the anachronism of the old Ghan actually lasted until the 1980s.

The crew on board the new Ghan still recalled the old one fondly on the evening I travelled north from Adelaide; I think most of them, even the younger men, would have gladly gone back to it. 'When we left home in Pirie on a Monday,' said one gaunt old hand, 'we used to say, "See you Friday". But you never knew which Friday it might be – the next, the one after or a month later. It was even worse before they built a standard-gauge line up to Marree in 1957 as it could take a couple of hours to do fifteen miles on the old narrow-gauge through Quorn. Then we crossed the platform in Marree to the Ghan proper and the fun began.

'I started as a waiter in the buffet car, which meant that after leaving Marree on a Monday night we served breakfast, lunch and dinner on the Tuesday and breakfast on the Wednesday morning before reaching Alice – if everything went to schedule, that is. We brought all the tucker up from Pirie for the journey there and back, but there wasn't a 'frig on the Ghan until the sixties, just blocks of ice which used to melt after a couple of days until we could get some more in Alice.

'We had two big coal-burning stoves in the kitchen and the cook had to be up at four-thirty, chopping up old tomato crates for wood to get 'em going and put the steaks on. It was that smoky in there we used to call him Al Jonson, and every trip someone had to climb on to the roof to clean the chimney out.'

Old Hand stopped to refresh himself. His beer can was wrapped in one of the white napkins left in our dining-car.

'I reckon it sometimes reached 150° in that kitchen. You couldn't wear a collar and tie in there, just a tee-shirt and handkerchief round your neck. Of course you weren't allowed a beer because railway rules said you could never drink on board – but they'd roll a five-gallon keg on all the same at Quorn. The inspector would get on there too but he'd never find it in that kitchen, that's how good they were at hiding it.'

When Old Hand started in the fifties the carriages came from Germany and had Rhine castles painted all over their interiors. They didn't have any air-conditioning, just a canvas water-bag at the end of each carriage from which to take a drink. Some of the diesel engines brought in about then came from Germany too, and he said they had the same sort of engine as the old U-boats. Later they built some carriages in Port Augusta which had battery-operated air-conditioners in the lounge-car and dining-car, but even then the dust and rain still came in round the window frames and passengers in the morning had their faces covered in grime.

'I had to go round every morning with hot water, for washing and shaving in, with a couple of watering cans like you have in your garden. "Have a shave this morning, sir?" I used to say. Had to do the shoes as well, which they left in a box outside the compartment door. I'd clean 'em if there was two bob inside; if there wasn't I'd leave 'em or put a bit of black polish on if they were brown ones.

'After breakfast I had to go round selling sweets and things down the train. There'd be two or three first-class and a couple of second-class carriages, and at the back you used to get all the old stockmen and boongs [Aborigines]. One day when I was about sixteen I went into the last carriage to sell my minties and one of 'em says to me: "Have a drink, go on, have a drink, lad!" And he was drinking metho – methylated spirits. I ran out of there with one hand on my wallet and the other on my minties and didn't dare go back.

'It was hot in summer all right, 140° in the water-bag, and the winds were freezing in winter: I reckon that was the worst part of it. But the floods were all right, something different; they made it into a regular mystery tour. We were never near starving or anything like that because these old bombers would come overhead as slow as possible and drop a load of canvas bags, which would burst and scatter meat and vegies all over the roof. The old boongs round Oodnadatta used to have a field-day then, picking up all the stray tucker.

'I've seen water thirty feet deep and quarter of a mile wide at the Alberga Bridge and several times we were stuck at Finke River. They built concrete pillars for a new bridge there, and – no bullshit – it collapsed the first time it flooded: a bloody great mallee was swept down, the water banked up behind and I reckon it must have undermined the whole bridge. We had to spend three days there once, waiting for the water to go down. Whenever we were stuck at the Finke we bought all the tucker out of the store and all the drink out of the pub, and the railway had to pay. That's why it never made any money – paying passengers' meals for a week or two instead of the scheduled couple of days.'

The conductor came round, and Old Hand wrapped the napkin more tightly round his can so that railway regulations wouldn't be seen to be broken. The dining-car had long since emptied after the evening meal. The new Ghan, locked and sealed, hurried over its concrete-sleepered rails.

'After a while of these bridges being washed away,' he resumed, 'they'd build the line straight through the water-courses. The trouble was that diesels can only go through two or three inches of water because if it gets into your traction motors you're in strife, whereas steam engines could be taken as far under water as they'd go. At least Lake Eyre never gave us much trouble, although I've seen waves coming over us like if you were by the sea. But then it started drying up and the dead fish were something – until the pelicans came along.

'For water we used to stop at William Creek, Edwards Creek, Finke River – anywhere we could water up. When we stopped at William Creek everyone climbed over the fence and went to the pub where they were supposed to sign the book saying they were bona fide travellers, though nobody did. And when the Ghan pulled out, if you were a bit tardy you had to run after it – which was all right, no worries, except if you happened to be carrying a dozen cans.

'By the time we reached Alice I reckon eighty per cent of the bloody township would be waiting to see the Ghan come in. They treated us like kings in those days – walking round amongst the stockmen in our black trousers and white shirts – "bringing civilisation to the outback", we used to call it. There must have been less than 5,000 people in Alice in those days. Now it's all changed. I don't think I've seen anywhere in the last twenty years that has changed so much as Alice.'

But it wasn't called Alice Springs when the first train arrived there – a mere five hours late – in 1929. That name was only applied to the nearby telegraph station. The township itself was known as Stuart until 1933, when the name of Alice Springs was given to the whole settlement to avoid confusion – and a soft feminine name for this oasis between two masculine-sounding deserts, the Gibson and the Simpson, has created a uniquely romantic appeal.

It is being cashed in on. When the number of legalised casinos in the whole of Australia was four, two of them were in Alice Springs. And it is the tourist centre for Ayers Rock, 200 miles away, frequently said to be the greatest monolith in the world but in fact not even the biggest in Australia. 'Come to Ayers Rock and watch its many moods from your air-conditioned room or at our slide evenings,' the brochures suggest. 'In the morning depart from Sunset Strip for a climb to the top of the Rock, sign your name in the visitors' book at the top, and explore the many caves sacred to the Aborigines. And try our Dreamtime Tours!

Learn all about Aboriginal life in half a day, see how boomerangs are thrown, be fascinated by Aboriginal people making traditional weapons and implements (afterwards you will be given an opportunity to purchase them!) and sample their bush tucker, before finishing off with a delicious barbecue lunch.' There is an airstrip beside this natural wonder; a tourist village for several thousands has been constructed behind some sandhills. Economically necessary, of course, as they no doubt said in the Temple.

Nevertheless, 'the Alice' itself has a pleasanter appearance than many outback towns. It has less neon, fewer wires and not so many bunting-strewn car marts. It has its ten-pin bowling alley and drive-in and video shops, but there are also casuarina trees clustering around the supermarkets, and anywhere that has casuarinas is redeemed in my view, not so much because of their countless shades of green in sunlight but because the wind soughing through them is my favourite natural sound. As well as the drive-in, a kind of film show is laid on every evening – free – by the MacDonnell Ranges on the town's outskirts: orange, russet, salmon – no word has been devised in the vocabulary of grey-green England to describe the lustre of those red-earthed hills at sunset. Yes, when the Ghan (new or old) noses through Heavitree Gap in the MacDonnell Ranges and almost passes down the main street of Alice Springs, arriving can for once actually better the traveller's hopefulness.

In the hotel I met Carole, a Californian tourist who had just been out to the Rock and reported the Land Rover trip was awful (feeling purist, I thought I'd either go there by camel or not at all). 'Awful,' she said again, with the loveliest female voice I've heard, having more of a flavour than an accent, 'which reminds me, I was in a Greek restaurant in Melbourne and on the menu it said "Lamb's fry". So I asked the waiter, "What is this lamb's fry, is it offal?" And he replied, "No, no, it's not – it tastes really nice."'

She was a marketing consultant, living in Djakarta, with a working knowledge of water buffaloes: Indonesia now wished to import some water buffaloes fom Australia, she said, even though they had originally come from Java.

Apparently, Indonesian buffaloes had gradually become flabby and infertile ('infertle') so that wild Australian buffaloes were required to improve the strain. Not that any water buffalo is truly wild: they are extremely placid, she maintained, and you have to go and shout at them to make them wild.

She had a wonderful cadence, in contrast to some Australian women who end every statement with an interrogative inflexion sounding like 'you know what I mean?' and which makes the listener feel an imbecile. Her conversation bubbled and flowed over abstractions and water buffaloes, over international politics and local prices, over whether Australia was more Americanised or Anglicised. The former, she believed: while Australia was English in tea and cricket, it was American in its business manner and desire for labour-saving gadgetry. More than that, she thought Australians were more Californian than Californians in that how they lived — their lifestyle — was more important to most of them than what they did.

We went to a bar one evening, where the customers sat on stools in shorts and tattoos. They were talking, as they swigged their cans, of those who spend their day sitting in the Alice marshalling yard or cross-legged under ghost gums in the dry bed of the Todd River. To them these Aborigines were 'rock-apes', 'coons' or 'boongs'. California Carole said their redneckery was reminiscent of the Deep South. But I feared there might be one sad difference: I doubted if these and others I'd heard were Klu Klux Klan extremists talking.

On the Indian-Pacific, for example, one of the conductors had given me his opinion about Aborigines. He was a late middle-aged fellow who had been brought up in Cook and gone rabbiting on the Nullarbor. Since then he had been a ballroom dancer, a pilot, a prospector as well as a train conductor, and he had suffered in the war at the hands of the Japanese: these people, he said, he could never bring himself to forgive after what he had seen, but he did respect them. Then he had delivered his view of Aborigines: 'I'd line 'em up against a brick wall.'

The wife of a hotel-owner in Adelaide had offered her

opinion. She was kind and friendly – said with a laugh she didn't mind I was a Pom. I had expected her to say something on the lines that Aborigines drank too much and some were lazy about finding work, but that there were some good fellows amongst them. Her opinion: 'I'd use the whole lot of them for target practice.'

This phenomenon among otherwise decent white Australians, most humane to their own kind but voicing feelings of hatred towards their Aboriginal countrymen, is of course nothing new. Back in 1883 the British High Commissioner in Brisbane wrote to Gladstone:

> The habit of regarding natives as vermin, to be cleared off the face of the earth, has given to the average Queenslander a tone of brutality and cruelty in dealing with 'blacks' which is very difficult . . . to realise. I have heard men of culture and refinement, of the greatest humanity and kindness to their fellow whites, talk, not only of wholesale butchery . . . but of the individual murder of natives, exactly as they would talk of a day's sport, or of having to kill some troublesome animal.

Yet the first white Australians, when they arrived from Britain, did not all bring this attitude with them – certainly not the leaders amongst them. At the time of settlement, Europe's intellectual climate had been shaped by Rousseau's notions of the Noble Savage, so that the instructions issued to the first governor, Phillip, were to treat the natives he encountered with respect. But other parts of Phillip's instructions emphasised that the primary aim of his expedition should be settlement: and therefore both sides were on a collision course from the start, for what the newcomer was determined to settle and cultivate, the native wanted to hold sacred and preserve.

This inevitability of a clash had been prophesied by Cook in 1770 when he wrote in his diary about 'the natives of New Holland': 'they covet not magnificent houses . . . they live in a warm and fine climate and enjoy a very wholesome air, so that they have very little need of clothing and this they seem to be fully sensible of . . . in short they seemed to set no value upon any thing we gave them.' So that while the white man has tended to covet magnificent houses, to feel that he needs clothing, and to work hard in order to amass capital with which to buy land, the semi-nomadic Aborigine works only with the aim of a bare subsistence and his great be-all, land, is not something that belongs to him but rather something that *he* belongs *to*. This has been observed numerous times. The tragedy, I suppose, is that Aborigines should have been confronted with a society whose values could not have been more diametrically opposed to their own.

However humane Phillip and succeeding governors were in Sydney, convicts in the field, having been treated brutally themselves, were liable to treat the natives likewise, although always there were honourable exceptions. Once it was fashionable in Australia to argue that diseases brought in from Europe, and to which the Aborigines had no powers of resistance, had been mainly responsible for the reduction in their numbers from an estimated 300,000 in 1788 to less than 100,000 by the turn of this century. But there must inevitably have been violence as the land of the south was cleared for merino sheep and later the north for cattle.

Resentments were unavoidable. What H. L. Mencken once wrote of the Negro could also apply to the Aborigine: 'one of the things that makes a Negro unpleasant to white folk is the fact that he suffers from their prejudice. He is thus a standing rebuke to them.' In addition to this aggravation of any white sense of guilt lingering from the past, the Aborigine is not grateful for what the white man has brought. It is like Israel. The modern colonisers of both countries justify their presence with the economic argument that they have developed their new-found land and increased its production ten- or a hundredfold. Yet, perversely in their eyes, neither the Aborigine nor Palestinian is the least bit grateful to the coloniser for making his desert bloom.

Perhaps this white resentment towards the original inhabitants was also partly a reaction born of frustration with the land itself. Settlers described how strange they felt in a country of such immensity and (to their vision) sameness, of aridity and silence, stocked so differently from home with trees that shed their bark not their leaves, and animals so peculiar that only the dingo was reassuringly familiar. Harmony between the newcomers and this land, let alone its original inhabitants, was bound to take generations to develop.

During my days in Alice I never saw a white person and a full blood in conversation. The only intermediaries were the 'mixed bloods' – not a term they themselves like. Once despised above all other creatures – maybe because they added to the white man's sense of guilt a reminder of his promiscuity – the mixed bloods now at least have the advantage of being able to feel at home in both time and place, in their own country and in the twentieth century. Xavier Herbert at any rate, in *Poor Fellow My Country*, advanced his belief that a mixing of white settlers and native women would have been the best means of populating the land. But I doubt whether the idea would be seen to have great merit in those pubs of Alice.

In the 1981 census, 3,000 people in Alice Springs classified themselves as Aborigines out of the 18,000 population. Yet they run into disproportionate trouble with the law (of the white man). There were 5,584 people taken into the police's protective custody in 1982: of those only 190 were European. And the majority of offences stem from drink, to judge from another statistic, namely that twenty out of every twenty-two cases admitted to the local hospital are alcohol-related. This, of course, is hardly surprising. Historically strangers to alcohol, the Aborigines had – and still have – no social or physical defence mechanisms against it.

A bonza place, Alice? Well, fairly bonza, on the surface at any rate, and the tourist anywhere is seldom tempted to look deeper. But it might have been wiser if it had stuck to its original name – Stuart. A Town Like Stuart? Then the reality wouldn't have to live up to so romantic an image.

4
Pine Creek to Darwin

'But the horrid thing in the bush! He schemed as to what
it would be. It must be the spirit of the place.'
(D. H. Lawrence, Kangaroo)

He was a Gabriel Marquez character, sitting under his felt
hat and a gum tree outside the only pub in Pine Creek. For
years he had sat there from nine each morning watching
the temperature and his tally of cans edge up towards the
hundred mark. During the afternoon he would be visited
under his tree by friends who had been with him on the
Sepik and gone 'troppo' in New Guinea; but in spite of
these friendships and the fidelity of the half-Aboriginal
woman who moved in a week after his wife had run
away and who kept his tin hut spotlessly clean, his closest
companion was the kookaburra that talked to him from
the gum tree spreading above his head. Occasionally this
tree would send one or two gum leaves floating down
beside him, and their moth-ballish smell of camphor would
remind him of the Christmases of his childhood in Sydney,
when he used to stand beside the clothes chest and close
his eyes, while his mother rustled inside to find her one
good evening gown.

His forehead was lined with creek beds that gradually
filled with sweat whenever he nodded off in the heat of the
tropical day. When he awoke he would shuffle inside the
bar to buy another stubby can, standing beneath the ceiling
fan to let the creeks run dry, before returning to his seat to
roll cigarettes and spin yarns of the life he had known in
the Northern Territory for over half a century. Or his mates
who had been out fossicking since before the sun came over
the scrubby hills would sit beside him and show him the

most promising quartz they had picked up from the old mine-shafts, littered though they were with shards of Chinese bowls and opium pipes as well as flecks of gold. Then he would squint through his pocket microscope, push his felt cap back and tell his mate he had as good as found El Dorado.

He reckoned that he himself had made half a million pounds – pounds, mind, not new-fangled dollars – out of Pine Creek gold. But he always allowed himself to be bought a stubby, since he had blown most of it on a dog in Sydney that had done the classic thing of sprinting miles ahead of the field, before veering off the track and under the rails. He had first come to Pine Creek in 1934 when a few Chinese still remained, working the mines and living in their troglodyte burrows. Some of course, as he said, had already been sent home by ship from Darwin, or been pushed overboard in shackles outside the harbour to save everyone's time. He remembered a few white miners as well in Pine Creek, although he always said their number was reduced by one after the Second World War when he was eaten unawares by local tribesmen, in spite of their preference for Chinese flesh that had been more tenderly raised on rice and vegetables.

What not even he could remember, however, was the time when a telegraph surveyor walked through the jungle and supervised the madness of stretching a telegraph wire across 2,000 miles of uninhabited country, simply in order that someone at the other end in Adelaide could hear taps and bleeps. That was in 1871 when Surveyor MacLachlan saw a glint in what is now Pine Creek and bent down to discover five ounces of gold. Down the wire the message went to Adelaide, whose Methodist citizens considered gambling to be diabolical but speculation on the stock exchange perfectly respectable. They immediately paid vast sums for gold-mining claims they had never seen, and would never see unless they were willing to take a ship to Darwin and then wade south through a bog for months – or else wait until the ending of the wet season.

It seems equally crazy that a railway should ever have been built at Pine Creek, but one was, even though it arrived from Darwin after the gold rush had moved on and the total white population of the new terminus town was down to no more than 100 people. It was known as 'the line that led to nowhere', and that remained the case even after it had been extended south from Pine Creek to Katherine and Birdum. The line was economic lunacy: when it was built, the number of people in the entire Territory totalled 1,009 (white people, that is: Aborigines were never counted in a census then, though they were allowed to ride in the trucks for three pence a mile). But some rusted rails near the pub, and an iron shed that once called itself Pine Creek Station, insist that the line really did once exist.

'The Palmerston and Pine Creek Railway' was its original title, although even then everyone knew Palmerston as Darwin. Two thousand Chinese were imported to lay the track at the rate of half a mile a day, with the assistance of mules from Uruguay. The earthworks were constructed by 800 men as brown as Aborigines, but not Aborigines, since the local natives used to be startled into flight by the great black buffalo that charged towards them spouting steam from its single horn. They were in fact built by Tamils who were sent back afterwards. The Chinese stayed, as Chinese do. It was never established what happened to the Uruguayan mules. Finally a tank engine was brought from Philadelphia to run along the line, and the Sandfly duly did so for many years, until derailed one day by a cow. Thereafter it was reserved for work on a nice and safe jetty in Darwin where no cows would ever molest it again.

There are few accounts of the Palmerston and Pine Creek, for the reason that few passengers ever went on it. But soon after the turn of this century Mrs Aeneas Gunn made a trip with her husband ('the Maluka') and she left a jolly account in *We Of The Never-Never*:

> From sun-up to sun-down on Tuesday the train glided quietly forward on its way towards the Never-Never; and from sun-up to sun-down the Maluka and I experienced the kindly consideration that it always shows to travellers: it boiled a billy for us at its furnace; loitered

through the pleasantest valleys; smiled indulgently, and slackened speed whenever we made merry with blacks by pelting them with chunks of water-melon; and generally waited on us hand and foot, the Man-in-Charge pointing out the beauty spots and places of interest, and making tea for us at frequent intervals.

It was a delightful train – just a simple-hearted, chivalrous, weather-beaten old bushwhacker, at the service of the entire Territory. 'There's nothing the least bit officious or stand-offish about it,' I was saying, when the Man-in-Charge came in with the first billy of tea.

'Of course not!' he said, unhooking cups from various crooked-up fingers. 'It's a Territorian, you see.'

'And had all the false veneer of civilisation peeled off long ago,' the Maluka said, adding, with a sly look at my discarded gloves and gossamer: 'It's wonderful how quietly the Territory does its work.'

The Man-in-Charge smiled openly as he poured out the tea, proving thereby his kinship with all other Territorians; and as the train came to a standstill, swung off and slipped some letters into a box nailed to an old tree-trunk.

At the far end of the train, away from the engine, the passengers' car had been placed, and as in front of it a long, long line of low-stacked sinuous trucks slipped along in the rear of the engine, all was open view before us; and all day long . . . the engine trudged onwards – hand in pockets, so to speak, and whistling merrily as it trudged.

Pine Creek, where Mrs Gunn dismounted to start her less jolly life in the Never-Never, is now the only gold-mining town in the Territory still alive, though breathing faintly. The railway families left in 1976 when the line 'ceased operations', but a company has recently moved men there to open up old mines, now that water can be pumped out of them by machine. If you approach their workings on a hill, a gun greets you at the gate; or you can meet these men in tattoos and vest in the pub every evening, when they drive away the Gabriel Marquez man by playing hard rock on the jukebox, as if they hadn't had enough of crushing it by day.

Strange things can happen in Pine Creek: shortly after breakfast one sultry morning I was busy lying on my bed reading Eyre's journal of his expedition from Adelaide to the west coast of Australia – the passage where he kept himself alive by wiping dew off the saltbushes with a sponge – when the hotel-owner's wife came in. She was dressed in nothing but a bath towel wrapped sarong-style around her torso. What was not covered by this sarong was revealed to be a bit like Australian wines: full-bodied and attractive, possibly even a trifle over-vigorous. In spite of the dehydrating heat, therefore, I sat up and forgot about the journey of epic Eyre-like proportions that I was planning.

I greeted her warily, however: 'Looks like a nice day for it.' After all, being Australian she might only have dropped in for a friendly chat, dressed in the informal Territory way. Besides, I reflected, a lot of men carry a gun in the informal Territory way, and quick calculations suggested that that number must include a large percentage of husbands.

'Nice day for a walk, I mean.' I decided to sound her out instead by posing as a follower in the footsteps of those heroic explorers of the nineteenth century who opened up this last inhabitable continent. I asked her whether the stretch along the railway from Pine Creek to Adelaide River would be interesting to walk; she replied there was nowhere on that stretch to stay the night, not a single house, and it was all of sixty miles. 'No worries,' I murmured non-chalantly.

Whereupon she regarded me closely: 'Someone like you would be more suited,' she said, 'to the Adelaide River-Batchelor section – that's sixteen rather than sixty miles. And if you want to find out a bit about this country first, talk to the old fella downstairs before doing anything bloody stupid.' Some Australian women, like the wines, can be refreshingly direct.

'And the vast, uninhabited land frightened him,' wrote

D. H. Lawrence in *Kangaroo*. Undoubtedly it did. On foot, I had left Adelaide River – as suggested by the hotel-owner's wife – at first light, since when the only sign of human life had been the rusted track and the telegraph wire (both seemed to hum but they were only cicadas). The sun had dried my shirt out, then soaked it again. I had no compass. If the track had just stopped or disappeared off the map, so might have I.

After two hours' march, towards eight o'clock I reached the only place between Adelaide River and Batchelor that was marked on the map, Stapleton Creek. (Stapleton had been the officer in charge of a nearby telegraph station until he was murdered by the Warramunga in 1874.) I saw the greenery surrounding the creek and heard its water flowing – seemingly heard it, save this was an audial mirage and there was no water. In the following hour I intended doing four miles before the late October sun fully heated up, but managed only three on heavily ballasted track. The bush became more tropical going north, the palm-like pandanus more profuse. Red and brown anthills growing to the size of a man were plentiful but in five hours of walking I saw no man, only two cars where a dirt road crossed the track and a distant farm – no other sign, apart from this track, that this land had been discovered.

When a wallaby thudded out of a thicket the two of us jumped equally high. A kookaburra laughed. Though the air was like a laundry my spine went cold when a scrub bull forty yards away looked up from its munching and started to charge, only swinging round at the last moment to head its horns in the opposite direction. The kookaburra laughed again.

'[The land] seemed so hoary and lost, so unapproachable,' Lawrence continued, transposing his feelings on to Richard Somers, an English writer of poems and essays visiting Australia:

> The sky was pure, crystal pure and blue, of a lovely pale blue colour: the air was wonderful, new and unbreathed: and there were great distances. But the bush, the grey charred bush. It scared him. As a poet, he felt himself

entitled to all kinds of emotions and sensations which an ordinary man would have repudiated. Therefore he let himself feel all sorts of things about the bush. It was so phantom-like, so ghostly, with its tall pale trees and many dead trees, like corpses, partly charred by bush fires: and then the foliage so dark, like grey-green iron. And then it was so deathly still. Even the few birds seemed to be swamped in silence. Waiting, waiting – the bush seemed to be hoarily waiting. And he could not penetrate into its secret. He couldn't get at it. Nobody could get at it. What was it waiting for?

... He walked on, had walked a mile or so into the bush, and had just come to a clump of tall, nude, dead trees, shining almost phosphorescent with the moon, when the terror of the bush overcame him. He had looked so long at the vivid moon, without thinking. And now, there was something among the trees, and his hair began to stir with terror, on his head. There was a presence. He looked at the weird, white, dead trees, and into the hollow distances of the bush. Nothing! Nothing at all. He turned to go home. And then immediately the hair on his scalp stirred and went icy with terror. What of? He knew quite well it was nothing. He knew quite well. But with his spine cold like ice, and the roots of his hair seeming to freeze, he walked on home, walked firmly and without haste. For he told himself he refused to be afraid, though he admitted the icy sensation of terror. But then to experience terror is not the same thing as to admit fear into the conscious soul. Therefore he refused to be afraid.

Is there some presence to be feared?

Plainly a fear of the bush must in part be rational for a white man who has not been trained to find water where it is invisible and cannot find shade where the leaves offer little. Moreover in the vastness, flatness and what is to him sameness, he can see no landmarks. He can find no escape because nothing is distinctive within his horizon by which he may take his bearings. Yet he expects things to be finite because he has been taught that God alone is infinite – but the bush is infinite too, in that he may walk as far as he possibly can and never come to any end but his own. That too is frightening, mystically as well as rationally: to be trapped in a sameness infinitely vast, without any heart or centre.

So why did Eyre and his fellow nineteenth-century explorers subject themselves to this fear and unreasonable hardship? It's a question not much studied, since these (in the main) Englishmen by birth have had little attraction for Australian scholars. But a pattern does emerge: if an identikit picture could be made of the typical Australian explorer it would depict a member of the lesser gentry of southern England, educated at a traditional public school, non-academic but ambitious, and not the first son or heir to his family's inheritance; therefore forced to make his own mark upon the world.

Perhaps the purest example was Edmund Kennedy, a third son, born in 1818 in Guernsey. His father was a colonel and his mother the daughter of a Lord Mayor of London. Educated at Elizabeth College on that Channel Island, Edmund was fully imbued with the contemporary Christian idea of service to God, King and Country – to judge by his later conduct and that of his brothers, who joined either the Church or Royal Navy. Edmund himself qualified as a surveyor and departed for Australia when twenty-one, characterised – according to his father's description – by an almost mad ambition to distinguish himself.

Kennedy never wrote much about his life but a friend noted that he was 'healthily uncomplicated, pleasant in every way, and the complete gentleman, by nature as well as by birth and upbringing'. So he did the honourable thing when he fell in love with an illiterate Irish girl, and kept Margaret Murphy and their child in funds – if discreetly elsewhere – while he went off to join the Survey Department in Sydney. There he kicked his heels: Sturt and Mitchell had opened up south-eastern Australia in the 1830s but a depression set in during the following decade, so interest in settling new land declined and with it the chances of doing some exploration.

Kennedy's big chance finally came when he was deposited on the coast of Queensland with an inaccurate map, and instructions to explore Cape York. He and his thirteen men hacked an epic path through mangrove, mountains and swamp until they were too bogged down to proceed further. Kennedy then decided to leave his men at a base camp and to set off with his Aboriginal guide, Jackey-Jackey, to find the relief ship meant to be waiting for them at the head of Cape York. But they were attacked *en route* by a notoriously aggressive tribe, their guns failed to fire after heavy rain, and Kennedy was hit in the back by a barbed spear – always fatal. Jackey-Jackey was thus left to reach the ship alone, and by doing so entered Australian lore as the archetypal 'faithful' Aborigine ever-devoted to his white master. He led the ship's crew back to the base camp where only two of the expedition had survived starvation. Kennedy himself, aged thirty, had died with an almost faultless reputation as an explorer and hero.

Charles Sturt also had a flawless reputation for a while after his death, but modern scholarship – mainly by an Australian part-time researcher, Edgar Beale – has put straight a record which Sturt's own imagination had improved considerably beyond the fact. Charles was a first son, but since his father had been the fifth son in a Dorset land-owning family and had received no share of the inheritance, the effects of lofty ambition and no money were similar. His father had left home to become a judge in Bengal, where Charles was born in 1795: sent back to England for a private education, he ended up at Harrow for his father did not have enough money to send him from there to Cambridge. Instead, Charles joined the army and had to wait nearly ten years after being commissioned as a humble ensign before he was promoted. When he finally became a captain, his regiment was sent to Australia to escort convict ships; but once arrived there Sturt found that an English gentleman even of his modest circumstances could act like a one-eyed king in a blind man's country.

With an amateur's knowledge of surveying Sturt headed west from Sydney in 1828 and found a new river which he named the Darling. Late in 1829 he set out again and made his famous journey down the Murrumbidgee – and back – in a whaleboat; he also came across another river which had already been named the Hume, but Sturt insisted on re-naming it the Murray to curry favour with another eminent figure. Soon afterwards he retired from the army and returned to Cheltenham to publish a two-volume history of his travels, *de rigueur* for every nineteenth-century explorer. But it was typical of Sturt that he should have pedantically entitled it *Two Expeditions into the Interior of Southern Australia, during the years 1828, 1829, 1830 and 1831* – the list of years being more impressive than a fair representation of the facts.

Sturt had a T. E. Lawrence tendency to exalt his own exploits – often under the guise of modesty – when there was no one's word but his own to substantiate them. It was the same when he wrote *Narrative of an Expedition into Central Australia*, after he had spent seventeen months discovering little but creating an heroic image for himself. 'No European in that respect had ever been more severely tried,' he said of his wanderings in the desert; 'no European living ... has seen so many of the Aborigines of the Australian continent as myself', which was almost certainly untrue, and unfair to Eyre.

It is not greatly surprising that Sturt has failed to convince modern Australians. Many would see this extract from *Central Australia* as plain 'bullshit':

> At noon I took a thermometer, graduated to 127°, out of my box, and observed that the mercury was up to 125°. Thinking that it had been unduly influenced, I put it in the foot of a tree close to me, sheltered alike from the wind and the sun. In this position I went to examine it about an hour afterwards, when I found that the mercury had risen to the top of the instrument, and that its further expansion had burst the bulb, a circumstance that I believe no traveller has ever before had to record. I cannot find language to convey to the reader's mind an idea of the intense and oppressive nature of the heat that prevailed.

No doubt Sturt suffered, and bravely too, but Australian

readers would know that a tree in the outback is very unlikely to shade a thermometer fully from the sun for an hour around noon.

Captain Sturt comes down as a very English man of his type. They are still to be found today, living in retirement, and not only in Cheltenham, as Sturt did: decent, fairish, formally religious and paternalistically kind to the natives; limited in humour and vision. He spent his last years trying to acquire for himself a K.C.M.G., while throwing up such a smokescreen of modesty that the *Australian Dictionary of Biography* says: 'Sturt allowed himself to be persuaded by his friends to apply for this distinction . . . he was personally always modest and retiring'. The hypothesis has even been advanced that he was victim of a mild form of paranoia and lived partly in his own fantasy world, but that is never going to be certified. Sturt was doubtless worthy, if long-winded, but never the 'father of Australian exploration' as he has been hailed by those who swallowed his propaganda.

E. J. Eyre, too, was a gentleman of far too modest circumstances for what *he* considered to be his proper station in life, who felt he had to rectify circumstances by becoming a hero. The third son of a Yorkshire clergyman, educated at Sedbergh among other schools, he had just scraped together the money to buy a commission when his father chose instead to send him to Australia. 'Although beginning life under great disadvantages,' he once wrote with feeling, 'I have ever maintained the character and standing of a gentleman.'

But Eyre was more than a status-seeker. He had a breadth of sympathy that led him to a deeper insight into the Aborigines than perhaps any white man before him. His only companion on his journey along the Great Australian Bight to the west coast was an Aboriginal, Wylie; and when Wylie met up with his fellow tribesmen again 'the cordial and hearty reception given him by his friends, and the joyous greeting bestowed upon him by all, might well have put to the blush those heartless calumniators, who, branding the savage as the creature only of unbridled passions, deny to him any of those better feelings and affections which are implanted in the breast of all mankind, and which nature has not denied to any colour or to any race'.

It is paradoxical that Eyre, the humane explorer, should have turned into a bloodthirsty executioner when he eventually became the Governor of Jamaica. There he took the concept of duty to God, Queen and Country to such extremes that he acted as an Old Testament God in ordering the death of 439 rioters. He appears to have been torn between both types of Victorian ambition – to serve selflessly as well as to serve himself.

While Eyre's journal (in two volumes) of his Australian crossing has been admitted as the inspiration for Patrick White's psychological portrait of *Voss*, it was the career of Ludwig Leichhardt that provided the outline of the plot. At first sight the tall, myopic, impractical Prussian seems the odd man out amongst Australian explorers but in social background he was not so different. He was the son of Christian Hieronymus Matthias Leichhardt, a royal inspector of peat-cutters officially, in practice a none-too-prosperous farmer. And, as well as being impoverished, Ludwig had the heroic yearning, expressed in a letter written on his east-west expedition shortly before he disappeared without trace in western Queensland: 'You know well that I consider Exploration of this Continent my great task, which has been allotted to me and which my previous studies have rendered me capable of executing satisfactorily. I consider consequently the persevering in this line of my life my duty . . .'

But the truly odd one out, and to me the most endearing of Australia's explorers, was the man who first circumnavigated the continent, named it, and provided some magnificent charts of its coasts, without seeking any medals or honours in return. Matthew Flinders, neither poor nor apparently very ambitious, was the son of a Lincolnshire doctor. He didn't blow his own trumpet, though he had more cause to than most, and no one since has adequately blown it for him. He did write the statutory two-volume narrative of his travels but he only got a copy in his hand the day before he died (at the age of forty), and he reserved his best prose not for his own achievements but for his ship's cat. Man has written few more tender tributes to a fellow animal. Whenever this cat was swept overboard it would climb back up the rope thrown out to it; and it would pose, like a 'lion couchant', in front of the crew in order to have its white paws admired. The journeys made by Flinders, at any rate, were not ego-trips.

Being neither a younger son nor a member of the minor gentry, nor a would-be hero, I found my walk hard going. There was no risk of hypothermia. After five hours without a sign of a cloud or of water or a human habitation, I saw a siding ahead and walked lamely into it. When another kangaroo bounded out of a thicket I was too foot-sore, from the ballast of crushed rock along the track, to jump. From the siding an aircraft hangar was visible, beside a runway which I discovered later had been used by bombers in the Second World War. I hobbled over to the hangar:

'Where have you sprung from, mate?'

'Adelaide River.'

'What, you've flown up?'

I was flattered. 'No, actually I've walked.'

'My oath, that's some way in this heat. You know it's the suicide season, don't you?'

Never mind, I had joined the ranks of Eyre, Sturt, Kennedy . . . After drinking large quantities and sitting under a shower for the rest of the day, I even worked out how my sixteen miles compared with the efforts of my predecessors. I calculated that I had done a fair proportion of one of those typical nineteenth-century expeditions: about one-thousandth.

Throughout its history of white settlement that northern part of the Northern Territory known as the 'Top End' has given an impression of being virgin territory, just waiting for the white man's seed and capital investment. The Top End has acquired the title of being Australia's last frontier, which suggests there's an Alaska or a Texas up there ready to be tapped. But while fortunes have been made, there have been many more bankruptcies, and that suggestion has not yet been confirmed.

Commercial schemes were the first to come to nought: attempts in the first half of the nineteenth century to create a second Singapore at various sites on the northern coast were killed off by poor anchorage and the unhealthy climate. Then MacLachlan of the telegraph spotted his five ounces: although the Territory's gold was soon found to be of 'poor quality and shattered by faulting', mineral extraction has come closest to being a success story so far, and still heads the list of the Territory's income-earners. Innumerable pastoral and agricultural schemes have been attempted also, like the 400,000 coffee plants which instantly withered; almost all these, except cattle farming, have proved unprofitable.

Considering the sunshine the Territory receives and the amount of rain which inundates the Top End each wet season, it is quite remarkable that the place has never been able to feed itself on anything but beef, and suggests incompetent administration in the years when the Territory was governed from afar. While Adelaide was in charge, the long-standing trade between the Macassans of Indonesia and the north coast Aborigines in trepang or sea-slugs (for Chinese soups) was killed off by over-taxing the Macassans. When Canberra took over, the Territory was too far away from federal consciousness, had no electorate to bear in mind, and hence was the first to bear any expenditure cuts. Only when Aborigines grew food in Alice Springs for the army during the Second World War, and costs didn't matter, has the Territory been near to feeding itself; and when Chinese kept Darwin supplied with the produce from their market gardens.

The constant lament of the Territory used to be that it was under-populated and therefore did not receive sufficient investment. However, there was something even more constant than that lament: xenophobia. Darwin, as Australia's nearest city to Asia, had the opportunity to become the meeting place of numerous cultures: Japanese pearl-drivers came there, Malays, Filipinos, Macassan fishermen and Chinese. But the white minority was fearful of being overrun and consistently discouraged this 'Yellow Peril'. Even more than the lack of capital investment, this self-inflicted shortage of foreign labour and talents may be considered to have held the Territory back.

The first Chinese to come to Australia in large numbers had arrived on the Victorian goldfields in 1855. They sailed from southern China in groups of six to seven hundred and aimed to earn enough to repay their debts at home in a few years. The cheapness of their labour brought them offers of employment from the mining companies and resentment from white Australians. The governments of Victoria and New South Wales therefore restricted their entry by sea. But more Chinese landed in Australia and walked across to the eastern states in single file, whereupon over a thousand diggers took the law into their hands and attacked the Chinese community at Lambing Flat. Subsequent 'justice' was so impartial that all the Europeans charged with rioting were later acquitted by juries in Goulburn. 'Two wongs don't make a white' was already a stale joke by the turn of this century; and so race hatred grew in the same soil as the ideal of mateship – mateship being restricted towards fellow Celts or Anglo-Saxons.

South Australia did not need Chinese, but did require them for its dependent Territory, initially for the Palmerston and Pine Creek Railway. The first shipload came from Singapore, then hundreds more from Hong Kong and the delta area around Canton. On the railway they were paid three shillings and sixpence a day; when it was completed as far as Pine Creek, they moved on to the goldfields round about and earned a wage of six shillings a day. White labourers on the other hand were paid five pounds a week, and even those high wages could not attract sufficient of them. So from the start Chinese hands were essential in the Territory if any work was to be done viably. Their low wages could make the goldfields pay; they could also make food production profitable. Chinese industry was the key to making the Territory prosper, and their presence would have been a defence in itself against the charge by expansionist Asian neighbours that Australia was allowing her land to go to waste.

By 1888 there were over 7,000 Chinese in the Territory, their peak in numbers; this compared with 1,009 Europeans; and at that point the Territory's population – not counting Aborigines of course – stood at its highest level until the Second World War. Besides mining and railway-building, fishing and market-gardening, the Chinese were active in tailoring, laundering, restaurateuring, trading and prostitution. A statistic survives, compiled by some diligent government official (never let it be said that Darwin bureaucrats weren't painstaking), to the effect that there were thirty-four Chinese prostitutes in Darwin in 1888.

With the economic depression of the 1890s some Chinese went home, but it was the climate of white hostility that was chiefly responsible for the reduction in their numbers to less than a couple of thousand. The South Australian government placed a poll tax of ten pounds on every Chinese entering the Territory and forbade them from acquiring any more mining leases. Furthermore the main union, the North Australian Workers Union, would not allow any Chinese members until the Second World War, so they couldn't get any jobs on the wharves in Darwin.

Joseph Conrad never visited Sino-Darwin (he only got as far as Sydney), and he must have missed a tale or two. There was the story about the opium cache: the Chinese inevitably smoked opium, and sold the left-over ash to Aborigines, but no one suspected that the aide-de-camp to the Government Resident would smuggle opium or keep himself above suspicion by storing it beneath the Resident's mattress! If not full of unspeakable mysteries, Darwin had considerable atmosphere before its Chinatown was destroyed in 1942, judging by this description in 1915 by E. Masson:

For the most part, the buildings are tailoring establishments, where hollow-chested Chinese boys sit all day whirring at their machines, or else they are laundries, where, through dark doorways, the owner can be seen swiftly ironing, or again they are stores. The stores are all alike – dark and smelling of incense and dust. Two seats of polished bamboo guard the door, on which old

Chinese lie and smoke, their knees drawn up to their chins. The shelves on the wall are covered with a curious collection of things – tins of biscuits, fans, tubes of toothpaste, bottles of aspirin and prints of Sun Yat Sen all mixed together. In the dark background are rows of fruit jars, big baskets, and solid cedar tables, while over all this presides the crudely painted image of the Joss.

With other Asian immigrants blended in, it would have been a rich racial mixture in the making – but that didn't suit many white Darwin citizens. Their attitude was best illustrated when the Chinese opened a night school and they complained that 'the Chinese already knew too much for the good of the whites in the Territory and if they were educated they would completely supplant all clerks and professional men'. So much for the open market; the White Australia policy, encapsulated in the 1901 Constitution, did not go far enough for some in keeping foreigners out.

After white commerce and white goldmining had failed to develop the Territory, sheep were transported to the Top End, there to be stricken by some indestructible tick. Cattle were introduced more successfully. But local conditions had first to be understood: on such land and in such a climate individuals could not succeed for long in cattle-grazing, only large companies that could survive the lack of any early returns on investment, the high white labour costs, the small local market and the lean years of drought until the eventual bonanza came along to make it all worthwhile. Foreign companies – initially British, latterly American – have long been dominant in the Top End and the neighbouring Barkly Tablelands: in 1909 Bovril Limited bought Victoria River Downs, said to be the world's biggest cattle run at 8,364 square miles. Then Vesteys, who had already been dubbed 'the princes of cold storage', moved into the Territory: they promised to build a meat-works in Darwin, employing local men, if Canberra – which had just taken over control of the Territory from South Australia in 1911 – agreed in return to extend the railway from Pine Creek to the cattle country around

Katherine and to provide all the necessary trucks and stockyards.

Here was a strange episode, involving Vesteys and the Commonwealth Administrator in Darwin, Dr J. A. Gilruth. In 1914, and again in 1916, Gilruth asked the Ministry of External Affairs (which governed the Territory then, as if it were a colony) whether they would be interested in selling off the whole Territory to a British company for five million pounds. No names were ever mentioned, but it just so happened that Sir William Vestey had stayed with Gilruth in Darwin shortly before the two offers were made. Conceivably, if the Ministry had agreed, a twentieth-century equivalent of the East India Company might have bought the entire Territory, and turned it into a cattle station the size of France and Spain combined.

Vesteys failed. The rail extension to Katherine was indeed completed by the end of 1917 (mainly built by, of all people, 223 Welsh-speaking Patagonians who were then deported); but the North Australian Workers Union made sure that aristocratic Vesteys did not flourish. Known for their militancy, its members held a monopoly control over labour in Darwin, and could cripple with strikes any overseas capitalists they didn't fancy. Vesteys built a meatworks overlooking the sea for the huge sum of nine hundred and sixteen thousand five hundred and thirty-three pounds, but had to write off the whole project following strikes and a slump in demand for canned meat after the First World War.

Thus, after the meat-works had folded, the Territory was left with a longer and even more uneconomic railway than before. It had been unprofitable from the first day of operations: it remained unprofitable even when services were cut to one train a fortnight each way. In railway construction there used to be an American rule of thumb that a minimum average of 200 people had to live in an area for every mile of new line passing through it, if that line were ever to make a profit. In the whole Territory there were twenty-five people for every mile of line when it was constructed in 1888; after a further extension had been added, starting in 1926, from Katherine south to Larrimah and Birdum, that average was reduced to nine white people per mile. This later extension was part of a Canberra initiative which saw the Northern Territory administratively dismantled and divided into North Australia (above Tennant Creek) and Central Australia. But nothing followed; there was no money for development and the old arrangement was restored in 1931.

Australia has the lowest population density of any land except Outer Mongolia, Botswana, Western Sahara, Greenland and French Guyana, having even today no more than two persons per square kilometre of surface area. That a relatively long railway should ever have been built in its most under-populated region, when the population was even smaller than now, may seem a preposterous notion – until those words of Sir William Jervois are remembered, concerning that 'Transcontinental Railway, about 1,800 miles in length, which will ultimately be carried through the Province of South Australia to Port Darwin'. Here we have the rationale. Economics and population were scarcely relevant: this railway was part of the colonial dream.

In partly fulfilling this dream by building the line north from Adelaide to Oodnadatta and from Pine Creek to Darwin, South Australia did as much as its finances would allow before handing over the Territory to Canberra in 1911. But there was a means of having a railway built in those days *without* paying out any money – the land-grant system. In 1903 tenders had been advertised in Adelaide for the construction of a 1,063-mile narrow-gauge line from Oodnadatta to Pine Creek in return for a huge block of 79,725,000 acres alongside the track; a minimum of 100 miles a year had to be laid by the contractor and at least one train a week was to run in each direction at an overall speed not less than twenty mph. But offers came there none.

So the South Australian government hurriedly sounded out several local syndicates, and revised terms were agreed with one of them. A single obstacle to this empire-building scheme remained: the syndicate wanted to use coloured labour. Asian workers had already been proved to be much cheaper and just as efficient as whites on the Palmerston and Pine Creek. The Commonwealth government however, adhering to its White Australia policy, refused to permit the entry of coloured immigrants to do this job. In consequence, since the cost of employing all-white labour was too high in Adelaide's opinion, the go-ahead for the line was never given. Australia stayed white; the Territory's development was set back half a century and more.

As the Channel tunnel has been to Britain and France, so has the north-south transcontinental been to Australia – a grandiose, all-but-impracticable pipedream that nevertheless refuses to go away. 'I do not believe I shall ever live to see a railway from Adelaide to Port Darwin or that even younger men than I will do so,'wrote Trollope. 'I cannot believe in the expenditure of ten million pounds on a railway which is to run through a desert and go nowhere.' Even so, as part of the terms of the Acceptance Act by which South Australia ceded the Northern Territory to the Canberra government, the latter actually undertook to complete this transcontinental railway. Only the time by which this had to be done was never specified.

There was an excellent opportunity during the 1920s, so much so that the question became not whether the line should be built but rather by which route it should go. A committee of inquiry traipsed round the major cities and compiled a vast report. Some witnesses insisted that the line should go directly from Oodnadatta through Alice Springs and on to Darwin since that was the route which had been intended, though not specified, under the terms of the Acceptance Act; others argued that in the wider interests of the whole country the line ought to proceed north-eastwards from Oodnadatta, thus opening up the far more fertile region of west Queensland (around Birdsville and cameleer Sedeeq's old stamping grounds), and linking there with the railways of the Queensland and New South Wales systems, before turning north-west to Darwin. These were both strong arguments. In the face of them the committee could only temporise, recommending a line as far as Alice Springs to placate South Australian opinion and reaching no conclusion about the transcontinental.

When the Second World War came, this indecision must have been regretted a thousand times. The Top End became, at last, the focus of national and international attention. It was Australia's front line against the Japanese. And Australians had no way, other than by air, of getting there once the shipping routes had been closed.

At nine-thirty-seven a.m. on February 19, 1942, warning was received in Darwin of the approach of unidentified aircraft. Although Singapore had collapsed four days previously, this warning was not treated with any particular urgency. At nine-fifty-eight, 188 Japanese carrier-based aircraft hit Darwin, bombing it far more ferociously than Allied propaganda ever admitted, not least because the government was so under-prepared that the total number of serviceable aircraft amassed at the local RAAF base to counter this attack was twenty-four. Those working on the wharves had little chance: one train was blown into the sea, 240 people were killed in the raid. It was the first of fifty air attacks on the Territory, which henceforth was more affected by the war than anywhere else in the country, until the theatre of conflict shifted eastwards to Guadalcanal and the Kokhoda Trail.

But the North Australia Railway, as the Palmerston and Pine Creek had become, was better prepared than the Air Force had been. Locomotives had already been brought in from narrow-gauge systems in other states and dispersed down the line, so that they could not all be knocked out in one raid. The line's finest hour was at hand: while the Ghan brought troops and equipment from Adelaide to Alice Springs, and the Americans built a road from there to Larrimah, the NAR was responsible for the Larrimah–Darwin supply route. Its rail headquarters were transferred from Darwin to Katherine, which besides having a delightful river was thought to have the advantage of being out of the range of enemy aircraft. It was found not to be: the Japanese bombed the rail yards and airfields, strafed repair gangs along the track. Nevertheless the line succeeded in increasing its performance by 6,000 per cent, from one train a fortnight before the war to 147 a week by 1944. Admittedly, some of the troops had to get out and push on the less gentle gradients, most had to ride in cattle trucks, and some of the locomotives were barely more than a sum of spare parts, so ingenious was the cannibalising of old engines; but the line did what its country asked of it. 'A highly satisfactory service forming a vital link in our defensive plan' reported the General Officer Commanding Northern Territory Forces.

After the war, however, gratitude was forgotten and the line was run down in accordance with those stupors into which Darwin itself relapsed. It was soon back to one train a week and a bit of shunting around the wharf – with a brief revival in 1966 when iron ore had to be transported from Frances Creek to Darwin for onward shipment to Japan. But like so many a Territory venture that one was boom-and-dust: a slump hit Frances Creek production about the time that a cyclone built up in the same area of the sea from where the Japanese had struck.

The natural disaster of Cyclone Tracy on Christmas Eve 1974 – when winds recorded 140 mph before demolishing the weather centre – was more devastating to Darwin than man's bombing. The financial cost alone was assessed at six hundred and fifty million dollars. The other damage – children woke up screaming for months after – was made worse, some psychologists thought, by evacuating three-quarters of the 46,000 population to tents, homes and caravans in the south: it would have been more therapeutic – if impractical – if they had stayed in Darwin to face their common adversity together. Be that as it may, the generosity of ordinary Australians was demonstrated to the full towards the victims. The government showered money on Darwin as if it were a bereaved cousin, suddenly recollected by guilty relatives after decades of neglect. Hospitals, highways and high-rise blocks were donated. But somehow there still wasn't enough to spend on an ailing railway, so the NAR's 206 employees were gradually assigned to other jobs. It would not have been politic to say they had been made redundant at that unfortunate moment or that the line had been closed; it was more convenient to say that operations ceased as from June 1976.

Given its solid new format of federal hand-outs and

cyclone-proofed roofs, Darwin has grown so fast that it has long outstripped its pre-Tracy size. It is the fastest-growing city in Australia, burgeoning with bureaucrats like a tropical Canberra. The remaining Chinese now run restaurants for those dining out on expenses. In 1966, two generations after white Australians had protested about the Chinese becoming educated, they elected Harry Chan to be mayor of Darwin. The pigtail, like Chinatown itself, has disappeared; there is intermarriage with Europeans, something unknown before 1936. Yet, demolished though the old city has been by natural and man-made forces, long-term residents say the old easy-goingness remains. The sea wrinkles and slides; the pace of living is governed by the humidity. Territorians, like their cars, tend to be big and slow. Darwin is even becoming a little international-ised. While I was there a second casino was nearing com-pletion by Federal Hotels Limited. It had been constructed on an Aboriginal burial ground where an elder of the Larrakeeyah tribe wept at the desecration. Containing a convention room for 350 people, a cabaret room for 350 more, and a VIP gambling area, the developers confidently predict their seven-hectare estate will become 'a tropical paradise'. (Oh yes, and an artificial lake has been created within the complex, featuring a little island dedicated to those Aborigines whose skeletons had been unearthed.)

And it's all for those Japanese and Chinese businessmen whose grandfathers White Australia was determined to keep out at the turn of this century. A second Hong Kong or Singapore is rising on the Territory's northern shore, belatedly.

5
Tasmania

'And then the mulberries! There was a lady in Hobart Town who sent us mulberries every day such as I had never eaten before, and as – I feel sure – I shall never eat again. Tasmania ought to make jam for all the world.'

(Trollope)

The first railway in Australia (the first *tramway* being a short line to carry coals from Newcastle to the sea) was constructed in Van Diemen's Land – as Tasmania then was. It was unique. Even Trollope would allow that a Tasmanian wasn't 'blowing' if he claimed the line to be a bit special. It was not its length, or gauge, or average speed, or its signalling system or the number of fishplates used that made it unique, but the means of traction. For this first Australian railway was not powered by steam or diesel locomotive, even by horses or camels or donkeys. Instead it called upon another resource with which the colony was exceptionally well supplied – convicts.

One St Patrick's Day in the 1830s Captain Charles O'Hara Booth was appointed Commandant of the Penal Settlement at Port Arthur in the south of Tasmania; and like his later compatriot Charles O'Connor, of the water pipeline that flowed uphill, Commandant Booth had a typically Irish brainwave. The voyage around Cape Raoul from Hobart Town (fine old Hobart Town – why did they have to drop the 'Town'?) to his settlement at Port Arthur had frequently to be made through rough seas; so he devised a short cut. He designed a railway line to go from Port Arthur to Norfolk Bay, which would enable passengers to make a far more sheltered voyage to Hobart. There were also coal mines on the shore of Norfolk Bay which had to be serviced by convicts, who were wasting much time by hacking a path there through the intervening bush.

Once the route had been established in his own mind and approved by the island's governor, Booth set his convicts to felling trees and clearing the way. These trees were used as timber for sleepers, rails and bridges *en route*: the sleepers were placed a foot apart, the rails were six inches thick.

All this is hard fact, but when walking round the ruins of Port Arthur an effort is needed to imagine the trains that once ran upon this railway, contemporaries of Stephenson's Rocket. Did they have first- and second-class seating? What was the buffet like? It is known though that the trains were limited to one carriage, and that each carriage – more like an open truck – had two seats across it (to carry four passengers normally) and ran on small cast-iron wheels. Three, or more often four convicts propelled it by seizing the bars extending on each side fore and aft and pushing the carriage forwards. Fortunately for them the line extended less than five miles and there was a change of crew halfway along the route. Unfortunately for them, the railway followed the lie of the land and had several steep gradients, which proved most arduous for the convicts to climb as they were always fettered with chains around their ankles, and most hazardous for the passengers to descend on the downward side. Estimates of the carriages' speed down these inclines varied from thirty to forty mph, a precipitous progress not exceeded by the nascent railways in England.

Upon reaching the top of a hill, according to one very Victorian account, 'the runners jumped upon the side of the trucks in a rather unpleasant proximity with the passengers, and away we all went, bondsmen and freemen, jolting and swaying in a manner that smacked somewhat too much of "the d---l take the hindmost" – although a man sitting behind contrived, more or less, to lock a wheel with a wooden crowbar when the descent became so rapid as to call for remonstrance'. About the only passengers known to have enjoyed both the sight of slaving convicts and the experience of hurtling carriages were – not perhaps surprisingly – a group of French naval officers who roared

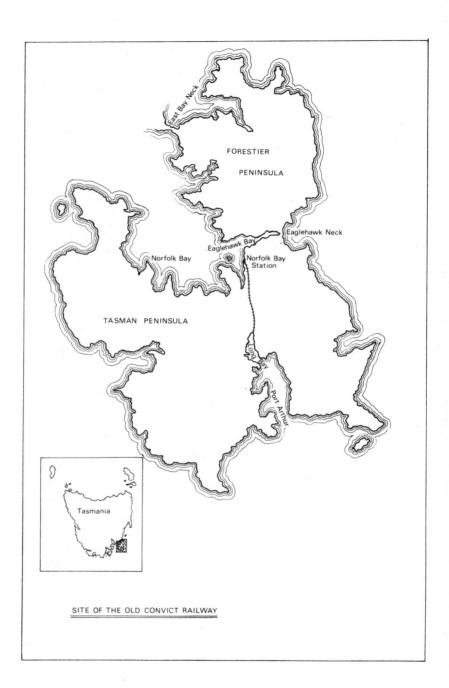

FORESTIER PENINSULA

East Bay Neck

Eaglehawk Neck

Eaglehawk Bay

Norfolk Bay

Norfolk Bay Station

TASMAN PENINSULA

Long Bay

Port Arthur

Tasmania

SITE OF THE OLD CONVICT RAILWAY

and bravoed their way downhill, ashore from their ship and doubtless drunk.

Some dour Victorian chroniclers tut-tutted at the brutality of this whole system, shocked that white men should be treated thus while slaves elsewhere were being liberated. But considering the other tasks that had to be performed in the penal settlement, I imagine that train duties compared favourably with swabbing down the penitentiary floors after breakfast or washing clothes or labouring in the sawmill on a freezing morning. It was really the whole convict system, not the railway itself, which was shocking. 'I must say that my feelings at seeing myself seated, and pushed along by these miserable convicts were not very pleasant. It was painful to see them in the condition of slaves which, in fact, they are,' wrote the Lieutenant-Governor, Sir William Denison, after his visit in 1847. 'It jars harshly against the feelings to behold man, as it were, lowered to the standards of the brute,' wrote a free settler. Yet what happened beyond their gaze at Port Arthur, behind the walls of the penitentiary, would surely have jarred yet more harshly.

On a fresh Tasmanian morning when the bright wattles were in bloom and the mulberries ripening, a convict's life must have come as near to being human as it ever did when he was attached to the ten twenty-six. Besides, there might be opportunities for self-expression which would not come his way under the jailers' eyes. As it will be remembered, although there was a brake on the carriage, it was not a very effective one; so that if the carriage were to be prevented from flying off the rails when rounding a corner at the bottom of the hill, the two convicts on the inside had to lean outwards as far as possible to steady the vehicle. If they did not, the carriage was liable to career off the track, and it would seem that the chance of derailing the train was often too attractive to resist, especially when some important personage was making the journey from Port Arthur to Norfolk Bay.

Thus it happened in 1843 that the Colonial Secretary, one James Bicheno, was in a carriage that flew off the rails. He received, it is recorded, 'tremendous concussion'. Now who is ever going to believe this was a complete accident? One smells another rat in the report that Commandant Booth himself was once ejected from a carriage. Moreover there was greater scope to the enterprise than merely inflicting cuts and bruises on those big-wigs whom the convicts did not care for. On another occasion an official was duly hurled into the undergrowth to cries of astonishment, and helped to his feet by kindly convicts who brushed the gum leaves off him most solicitously. Not till later did the official realise that his watch and purse had gone.

In spite of these 'accidents' the Commandant thought his line a great engineering triumph – it could also convey goods, half a ton per wagon – and his successors allowed it to continue until the ending of the Port Arthur settlement in 1877. Two additional convict-powered railways were operated as well, both shorter and nearer to Hobart Town. One was at East Bay Neck; the second crossed Ralph Bay Neck, where convicts had to push carriages through the shallows in order to save lady passengers from getting their feet wet.

Savage though Port Arthur was as a penal settlement, it must have been a holiday camp in comparison with its predecessor, Macquarie Harbour, on Tasmania's west coast, where the Roaring Forties strike land after a wild expanse of ocean and rain pours down on average 300 days a year: those sent there called the entrance to it 'Hell's Gates'.

The convicts sentenced to Macquarie Harbour were those who had committed a second offence since arriving in Van Diemen's Land. The penal records – studied with growing curiosity in Australia these days as it becomes respectable to trace a convict ancestry – make it clear that not many offences were serious, either those committed initially in Britain or subsequently in Australia. Thus such a case was William Jones: 'aged twenty years, found guilty at Old Bailey of stealing 1 handkerchief, value three shillings, sentence, transportation for life'.

Until the American Revolution, about 500 convicts a year were deported from England to the United States. But by the 1780s the numbers awaiting transportation had grown, English society having become ever more disturbed as a result of the Industrial Revolution and Enclosure Acts. A threatened Establishment made over 200 crimes punishable by death; and over the years 168,000 people preferred to have their death sentences commuted to transportation to Australia. (Tasmania took convicts until 1853; Western Australia, the last state to receive them, until 1868.)

Out of this mass of convicts the ones who had committed further offences in Tasmania were those dispatched to become the first white people to live on the west coast. In 1822 soldiers and prisoners sailed through Hell's Gates to begin one of modern man's most sadistic enterprises. To appreciate the brutality you have to see Sarah Island, where the penal settlement was based. Sarah Island has the remains of two shipyards where prisoners made brigs and boats out of huon pine. But first they had to row up the Gordon River to wade along the bug-infested banks and cut down this most ancient of trees ('the oldest living thing on earth', the huon pine – another 'blow'?), before lashing the logs together and towing them down river to Sarah Island in the evening.

Sarah Island, however, was the good news. Far worse was Condemned Island, a nearby rock, to which thirty or forty men were sent every night (the few women convicts were not wasted there) and left to sleep in chains, their clothes soaked by wading ashore. A surgeon testifying before a parliamentary committee on transportation in 1838 thought these convicts had been 'degraded', by extensive use of the extra-heavy cat-o'-nine-tails. Several convicts murdered anyone they could lay their hands on to achieve the soft option of being returned to Hobart for one good meal and hanging. Others made the mistake of escaping into the rainforest. Now, a government geologist once travelled hard for twenty-five days just to walk the last fifteen miles to Macquarie Harbour, mainly because of the plant called 'horizontal' which grows vertically, then keels over and creates a false floor in the forest through which the unwary disappear. Convicts who voluntarily went back to Sarah Island, grateful to be taken in again, were often found to have survived in the rain forest by eating their fellow-fugitives.

The most vivid description of Macquarie Harbour brutality was written by Marcus Clarke who, although he never went there, wrote the magazine serial that was abbreviated and published posthumously as *For The Term Of His Natural Life*. Though parts of his wild plot are more Gothic than realistic, without being a good book it was Australia's first great one.

As for Sarah Island today, it's too cold to spend a penny there, let alone a ten-year sentence. No wonder Flinders wrote on his circumnavigation (and how his poor cat must have shivered): 'Judging from appearances, the west coast of Van Diemen's Land is as dreary, and as inhospitable a shore, as has yet been discovered.' It certainly held no attractions for Abel Janszoon Tasman who first saw it in 1642, and sailed on, even though his compasses fluctuated suspiciously on passing two peaks not far inland.

Yet within seventy years of Macquarie Harbour being abandoned as too inhuman a prison (1833), here – in the coldest part of Australia, covered with sodden rainforest, mud and gorges, snakes and leeches – there were eight railway companies operating. Only one thing could bring about that transformation: mining. It was the same pattern in Tasmania as everywhere else in Australia.

At Mount Bischoff in the 1870s was discovered the world's richest tin mine (there she blows!). In 1882, beneath one of the mountains which had made Tasman's compasses unsteady and which had been given the name of one of his ships, *Zeehan*, silver was found. And over the next mountain range in the following decade copper was found, sufficient to make the Mount Lyell mine the biggest producer of copper in the British Commonwealth (here we blow again!).

A single one of these railways survives: the first of them happens also to be the last. It began as a horse tramway not much more sophisticated than that convict line, leading from the port of Burnie (or Emu Bay as it then was) to the mine at Mount Bischoff forty-four miles inland – and was therefore 'the longest horse-powered tramway in the empire' (!). Later it was extended south to Zeehan, steel rails were laid on a three-foot-six-inch gauge, steam engines were brought in (many of them that pushme-pullyou engine like a wheeled palindrome, the Beyer Garratt) and it became the privately-owned Emu Bay Railway. Its *confrères* have all gone, but the Emu Bay continues, though you have to be up early to catch the last passenger-carrying service in Tasmania.

It leaves Burnie every weekday morning at five o'clock (which is arguably the best time to see industrial Burnie, before daylight). You can imagine what the horses felt like climbing up the one in thirty-seven gradient out of Burnie since it takes five Class Eleven diesels to pull only twenty-seven empty ore wagons – along with however many passengers who care to fill the two spare seats in the guard's van. The train snakes in five different directions at times before reaching 2,000 feet and the plateau, where it enters a world of Reverend Awdrey-innocence.

It weaves along at twenty to thirty mph between hay fields and pastures, bungalow gardens and ponds, past ferns and – rarity in this country of fences – hedgerows. In Australia, Tasmania alone has the loveliness of English pastoral. People smile in their gardens and wave as the train goes by, while the guard waves back and tosses their morning newspaper to them. There's an echo of that nostalgia for lost innocence to be found in Awdrey's books, heard here in the names of small towns borrowed from the original homeland like Somerset, Hampshire and Guildford. There is also, however, the settlement of Que along the way: supposedly the 600 navvies working on the Mount Bischoff tramway gave it its name by queuing up for the brothel there.

Then the Emu Bay Railway disappears into forest. First it is sombre, dank, imported pine forest, planted since the war by the Forests Commission for pulping into newsprint. Thereafter native forest takes over for as far as the island extends south, except for those parts demolished by the Hydro Electric Commission. There's gum and myrtle, blackwood and celery-top pine; best of all, these trees have a tinge of brownness which makes their greenness richer. Celery-top pines have russet tips to their needles; trunks of the blackwood carry a deep dark moss. The gum tree may not give man enough shade for comfort, but at least its too-thin leaves do allow sunshine to filter down, setting the browns and greens of this native forest alight.

Ravines begin, and bridges over streams flowing west, and cuttings canopied by the forest. Only in this area of Australia are trains affected by snow; and it is also reputed to be 'Tiger Country', though there is no scientific evidence that the Tasmanian Tiger survives. Officially the last authenticated example of this animal – being a marsupial it has no genetic relation to the feline tiger, only a visual one, with dark stripes on its back – expired in 1936 at Hobart zoo. However, romantics feel that if any survive they will be found on this uninhabited stretch of west coast, and indeed in 1961 a tiger was flimsily reported to have been captured by two bushmen in the region to the west of this stretch of railway, between the Arthur and Pieman Rivers. But rainforest was never the tiger's preferred habitat, since it was built for running down its prey on plains or in coastal scrub. It had powerful jaws, which meant it quickly tucked into the merino sheep introduced by early settlers, which in turn meant it quickly had a bounty put upon its head. So Tasmanian Tigers were trapped and shot and poisoned, until the world's largest carnivorous marsupial (no blowing) had to be considered extinct.

Likewise that other hunted creature, the Tasmanian Aboriginal – although he might have survived on this west coast, but for the misguided philanthropy of one George Robinson. Back in 1830, Robinson went round the island persuading its native inhabitants to give up both themselves and their pagan beliefs (not to mention the potentially rich arable land they occupied in the east), in order that they could then be dispatched to happy Christian homes on Flinders Island. Once there, most of them died. But one group had remained on the western shore, living on seafood, 'fine looking men, five feet nine inches to six feet in height, well proportioned and broad shouldered', wrote Robinson. They built rafts for visiting off-shore islands, and permanent huts – not temporary bark shelters as on the Australian mainland – and covered themselves with animal fat and ochre to keep warm. Robinson therefore thought it his Christian duty to round them up as well and move them to Flinders Island in 1842, where disease and spiritual dis-ease killed off the last of them. But Truganini was not the last Tasmanian Aboriginal, as so widely believed. Their mixed-blood descendants live on, for white sealers who hunted off the Bass Strait islands captured some of their native women and took them over to Kangaroo Island off the coast of South Australia.

It is appropriate therefore in a poignant sort of way that Tasmania's last passenger train should survive on this west coat. Then shortly before the Pieman River, at Farrell Siding, the guard pointed out to me signs of an old track branching off through the undergrowth to Tullah where silver-lead was once mined. There, deep in the forest, the Tullah community used to be as isolated from the world as Cook, and again the railway was its sole link with the outside. Until 1962 when the first main road in the region was made, everyone and everything bound for Tullah had to take the Emu Bay Railway to Farrell Siding and from there ride a further six miles on the two-foot gauge line. 'It is doubtful whether a railway ever ran through a more rugged country and through such dense forests,' says the author of *Railroading in Tasmania*. At first a horse did the pulling on wooden rails; then a steam engine was bought just before the First World War, steel rails were laid and for half a century Wee Georgie Wood puffed up and down the line twice a day. There were actually two engines of that name, as the original one tumbled down a ravine (nobody was killed) and a successor had to be brought from a sugar plantation in Queensland. But they blended together and became one in the affectionate memory of Tullah. He – it was always 'he' – would sound his whistle in a specially rehearsed warning signal to the inhabitants whenever policemen thought fit to visit Tullah. He took all the silver-lead concentrates out of Tullah and brought in all the supplies for its one hotel, one school, one store and one mine. Over the years Wee Georgie Wood did the equivalent of ten journeys around the world – at a steady pace of six mph. Not surprisingly the community refused to sell him when the end came, but chose to preserve him in a shed alongside the iconoclastic road – in the making of which he had been indispensable.

From Farrell Siding the Emu Bay Railway descends to and crosses the Pieman River, lately turned by that controversial body, the Hydro Electric Commission, into a reservoir said to be more than twice the size of Sydney Harbour. Three days a week it stops on the other side in Rosebery to collect zinc-lead for the return to Burnie, and twice a week it continues a few miles further south to Melba Flats where copper concentrates from Mount Lyell in Queenstown are brought by road. A rusted track still leads on from Melba Flats to Zeehan, but no trains have run along it since the sixties. The line is derelict, like much else in the area.

One of the surprises of Australia is that so young a country (in terms of its white settlement) should have so many towns which have come, already been and long since gone. Of these the most remarkable in Tasmania is Zeehan. Its silver rush attracted over 10,000 people and made it the largest town on the island at the turn of the century, after Hobart and Launceston. There were twenty-six hotels, a thousand-seat Gaiety Theatre, a School of Mines and Metallurgy affiliated to the University of Tasmania, and a station with services on five different routes. The railways brought to Zeehan (because there were no roads) theatrical troupes, circuses, prize-fighters, brass bands and Houdini himself. Its Australian Rules football team was unbeatable – at least at home on their own ground where the surface was pebbles and pieces of silver-lead which stuck in the skin for a week.

The boom began in 1888 and lasted until five million pounds' worth of silver had been extracted from Zeehan – peanuts compared with Broken Hill but sufficient to give the west coast a kick-start towards development. Some of the subsequent changes can be plotted in back numbers of *The Zeehan and Dundas Herald*, kept in the Gaiety Theatre that is now a museum. On September

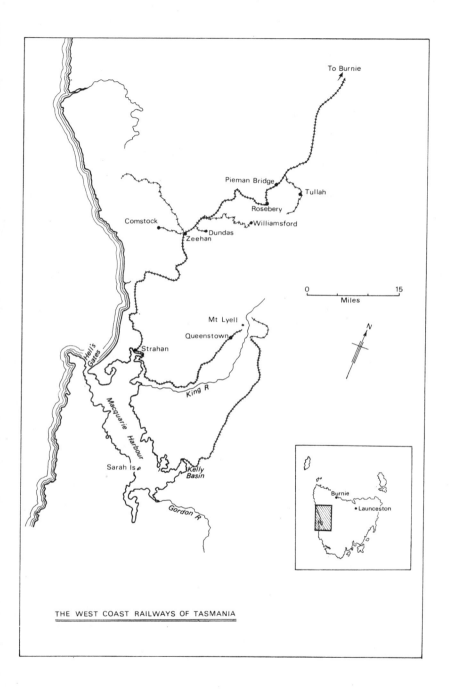

THE WEST COAST RAILWAYS OF TASMANIA

7, 1888, at the start of the silver rush, its front page was advertising stock- and share-brokers; and miners' essentials like 'Best Mole Trousers, 7s 6d' and 'Best Oil Coats, 16s 6d' as proof against the 300 yearly days of rain. 'Always see that your dynamite is "Sun" brand', one advertisement says, competing with another proclaiming 'Nobel's, the oldest Dynamite Factory in the World – Genuine Nobel's Dynamite, Detonators, Fuse, etc, kept in stock'. Life was rugged: Zeehan then was a load of shanties built on mud and optimism beside a bog of a main street, and a man's cheek was as rough as his boots.

Again it was the railways which were to make life almost tolerable. The Emu Bay Railway from Burnie and the opening of a new government line from Strahan to Zeehan (which was to fight a losing battle with sand dunes) ushered in a more gracious existence. Thus by May 1, 1899, the *Herald*'s front page was filled with: 'Going Fast – Button and Sly's 1s 11d Four-Button Kid Gloves, and no wonder, when they are well worth 2s 11d'; or 'Ladies' Wool Under-vest, 1s each'. W. T. York's, the big trading store just past the Gaiety, was meanwhile offering 'Ladies' Watertights, 9s 6d and 12s 6d. We have a nice assortment of Children's Lace and Button Boots'.

To convey customers to these stores, believers to the churches of various denominations, and students to the School of Mines, trams ran along the two-mile main street. By night auctioneers sold shares in the light of kerosene lamps; a roaring trade was done in the pubs and billiard parlours and no doubt, by the early hours, in the Zeehan and Dundas Hospital as well. Daily trains went north to Burnie, south to Strahan; and to Comstock, Dundas and Williamsford on two-foot tramways. Two extraordinary engines were delivered from Manchester in 1909 for the North-East Dundas Tramway, with cylinders at each end: the first Beyer Garratts to be commercially employed any-where in the world. And all gone now.

Suddenly the silver ore ran out. Young men went off to war, and returned only as names on the Anzac memorials. Most of Zeehan is a ghost town now, though Australia is a place of spirits more than ghosts.

One wonderfully fresh Tasmanian afternoon, when the unbreathed air coming off the great southern ocean was almost drinkable, I went to find the old station yard where engines clanked and shunted and clanged their bells until the last of them sounded its own knell in the early sixties. I cycled down the crumbling main street, past the old Gaiety and the former School of Mines, along where the trams went, and turned away from the base of Mount Zeehan to the former station yard. Some rails were hanging into the water from a bridge. From it, in one direction, a low embankment ran north through the valley to Rosebery. In the other, what had been the home for the first Beyer Garratts had been bull-dozed and turned into a housing estate, not a vestige of engine sheds left: just brightly painted bungalows. But, animated by that sun and air, I thought I could see again those steam trains, whistling, puffing, panting, back in the days of ore.

Queenstown, twenty minutes over the mountains by road (or, before the road came, six hours away by train) is a bit like a dream too; or a nightmare. In Queenstown, or 'Copperopolis', man produced the weirdest landscape in Australia. It is as if the surrounding hills had contracted scurvy, and every bit of their foliage had fallen out. Then jaundice followed, turning all this baldness yellow.

Sulphur killed those hills: enough to make 120,000 tons of sulphuric acid was belched over Queenstown in the days when nobody knew what the word ecology meant. It didn't matter what happened to men's lungs, or to women's laundry when hung in the valley behind their rows of tenement cottages. Laundry could be replaced – men too, for that matter. But the hills suffered irredeemably from the sulphur, and from being stripped of their trees to provide fuel for the smelters. Bushfires came to burn off their peaty turf, and the remaining soil was blown away by the Roaring Forties to leave the land naked.

Some residents of Queenstown like their lunar landscape and don't want vegetation to re-grow on their extraordinary hills. But I don't think it is possible to like Queenstown itself: it's a run-down company town where the only real status-symbol is the newness of your car. Yet its people have a sense of togetherness that's very like the spirit of the Welsh mining valleys; it can hardly be a coincidence that the most popular act in Zeehan's Gaiety Theatre, even more so than Dame Nellie Melba's, turns out to have been that of the touring All Male Welsh Choir.

Smelting lasted in Queenstown from 1896 to 1969, and it was an American employee of the Mount Lyell Company, Robert Carl Sticht, who pioneered the process of pyritic smelting and thereby – in using the iron and sulphur within the ore itself as fuel for the furnaces – reduced the amount of coke required to an economic level. Once Sticht had insured the profitability of copper-mining with this process, rivalry broke out between his Mount Lyell Company and the North Lyell Company on the other side of the mountain. Both built smelters and company towns, and their own railways up from Macquarie Harbour. And only after the North Lyell Company had effectively made itself bankrupt in 1903 by its extravagances (like stocking its railway with Pullman carriages), was it taken over by the Mount Lyell.

Queenstown had its mining disaster too, when a fire broke out in the North Lyell mine in 1913. Forty-two men were soon killed by the flames and fumes of carbon monoxide. But fifty-one survived further down the shaft, and they could be saved with the appropriate helmets and oxygen appliances. A ship from Melbourne brought the helmets to Burnie, from where one train rushed them to Zeehan and another on to Queenstown, five hours faster than normal schedule; and the men were rescued, after four days down the mine.

There is only one way to see these old lines. In Queenstown I hired a small plane, with a tall and elegant, recently-qualified lady pilot thrown in. She thought the exhilaration of flying derived more from the scenery you flew over than from the act of flying itself, and she must have a run to enjoy as exhilarating as anywhere. We flew over and down the former North Lyell Railway, its narrow-gauge track long since removed but its course still traceable through most of the bush and down to the port at Kelly Basin, and from there she headed across Macquarie Harbour.

It was one of those days of the year not among the wet 300. Down below, Macquarie Harbour was its unique almost-ebony colour, stained dark by the juice of huon pines and other trees that pack the banks of the Gordon. Hell's Gates and the terrible ship-wrecking bar were in placid mood; Sarah Island and Condemned Island floated on the dark glass as we passed over and up the Gordon River. Only the shadow of our plane, moving over the rainforest, was wrong, an eyesore. Everything else within our wide horizon was utterly unspoilt, unchanged by man, purely natural. No one tree, or mountain, or stretch of ebony water, was in itself miraculous; it was the unspoiltness, or rather the totality of it, that was so beautiful. To dam the Gordon below the Franklin River would be an assault on one of the last virgin territories.

Curving round, my pilot headed the plane back over Strahan towards Queenstown. The path of the old three-foot-six-inch Mount Lyell was plainly discernible along the banks of the copper-coloured King River, across a wooden trestle bridge that had collapsed and up the steep incline out of the gorge that had been conquered with four and a half miles of Abt rack-and-tooth railway. One Saturday in 1963 the last train ran; on the Monday they started taking the track up. But if only it had been preserved as a tourist attraction, the line could have provided ample employment for Queenstown in place of the dam project, without the fifty million dollars that the Australian Labour Party was then suggesting be spent on re-opening it.

The last passenger train on Tasmanian Government Railways was the Tasman Limited which ran from Hobart to the north-west of the island until 1978. By then its system had declined more than any other state's, owing to a difference of gauge between Hobart and Launceston, worn-out track, scant investment, the motor car, exceedingly slow trains and bureaucratic in-fighting (along with in-breeding, alas, a Tasmanian speciality). Australian National Railways took over, and with drastic pruning finished all passenger services, streamlined the system to a few main routes, and concentrated attention on timber traffic. Their policy has paid off; freight trains can take as long as they like to wend their way down to Hobart through the lowland Scottish countryside of the east coast, and the island's railways are making a profit.

Hobart today is dominated by Mount Wellington and unemployment. The former is one of those innumerable mountains or ranges of hills of which it is locally said: 'If you can see it, it's going to rain, if you can't, it's already raining.' Unemployment looks no less permanent, and drives many to leave the island and try to make it on the mainland.

But this manpower drain does not appear to affect the size of the young multitude, the generation largest in Australia's population, that floods every weekend to the Wrest Point casino complex that dominates the Hobart horizon. Its roulette tables cater more for visitors to the island, but the discos and bars are filled in the main by Tasmanians themselves – generally recognisable by being shorter than mainland Australians with lower brows and darker hair, and like some New Zealanders they may sport, sideburns that have long since disappeared from European fashion. Here they assemble in white silk shirts and mascara'd eyelashes for a night of escape into the international world of funk and soul, but in Tasmania there are in fact few of the excesses of mainland hedonism. The casino apart, it is a more restrained place, less hard-selling, almost Scandinavian – a cold-climate culture fitting naturally into a cold-climate country.

Both Hobart and Launceston are more rooted in the past than mainland cities. Perth and Brisbane are newer; old Sydney has been disembowelled and re-filled with high-rise; central Melbourne is all shops and offices; Adelaide comes closest to Hobart in being a city that you can walk around, but it still cannot quite match Hobart's air of settled permanence. Hobart's theatre and real tennis court (one of two in the southern hemisphere) and its early Victorian stone architecture are a relief from tile, brick, fibro-cement and bunting-strewn car marts. Especially fine is the wharf area, which has been preserved, unlike some of Tasmania's heritage – even a little over-preserved perhaps, to the point that shops carved out of the old warehouses bear names like 'Concept' and 'Lifestyle' – 'carts and rafts' shops offering tourists home décor in huon pine. Still, better to err that way than the other, and if you stand on the wharves one summer's evening when the last of the light lingers behind Mount Wellington and the eternal winds of Hobart scud Mussorgsky-like across the mountain, the thought may occur of that patronising phrase: 'Oh yes, a lovely place to visit, though I wouldn't like to live there.' But I wouldn't mind a holiday, at any stage of life, in Hobart – or, for preference, Hobart Town.

6

Melbourne

'An Australian does not see sport as the subject for an elegant essay; nor is he haunted by doubts that time spent playing games may be time wasted. He likes sport and that is all there is to it. And if he likes you, he will call you "Sport". He can think of no friendlier word.'
(Ian Bevan, editor of *The Sunburnt Country*)

Christmas in Melbourne: the time and place to think ahead to the New Year and the future. Thus far my journey had led through what people would broadly think of as 'the real Australia' – the outback, the bush, the Never-Never. But that is not where the majority of Australians live. They live on the east coast, in a line – or alongside the railway line – that stretches from Melbourne to Sydney to Brisbane to Cairns. This is where my trail now had to head, and furthermore, travelling up the east coast would mean a change in time as well as space. Until now, the train journeys had tended to lead into the past; henceforth they would touch more upon the present – and Australia's future.

First, though, an observation on the near-paradox that most people travel light on Australian trains, yet end up heavy.

Travelling light is something to be learnt by experience: Evelyn Waugh's hero in *Scoop* burdened himself with trunks and boxes and a tent and canoe because he had never been abroad before, certainly not to Abyssinia. But with practice comes wisdom: the more you travel, the less you realise you need. And most Australians, whether heeding this lesson or disdaining material effects, travel with remarkably little. Indeed, in an international table of luggage-carrying they would come at the top, travelling lightest – at the opposite extreme of Indians who seem to think that bedrolls and kitchen sinks are indispensable items in every educated person's baggage ('I have sink therefore I am').

Yet while going huge distances on Australian trains, one quickly becomes far from light oneself. Exercise is not readily available, food is: steaks and potatoes, wine and beer, and all one can do is sleep it all off. Only once have I found it easier to put on weight, and that was on an Italian ship which sailed through the Mediterranean and Red Sea heavily ballasted with pastas and antipastos. There were seven courses for every lunch, eight for every dinner. Australian trains only serve three, but in enforced idleness they were enough.

As opposed to the 'how' of travel, the 'why': well, for a start one takes to the road or rail for the intrinsic interest of seeing places, and every country on earth must be worth one month's stay, Australia far more. But, beyond that, the whole purpose of travel? The realisation, I suppose, that the grass is not significantly greener anywhere else; that while it is better to travel hopefully than arrive, it's better still to arrive home; that the philosophy 'East west, home's best' is as true as it is succinct.

Lastly, there's the observation – long since made – that the character of a people is often laid bare by sport. Reactions then are spontaneous and uninhibited; or as Paul Theroux put it, 'the muscular ritual of sport was always a clear demonstration of the wilder impulses in national character', citing how the British finally overcome some of their self-restraint when watching football. But in Australia that muscular ritual, which like paint-stripper reveals the essential underneath, has to be cricket. For there are no social niceties here, as in England: people play it to win.

Spencer Street Station was quiet on Boxing Day, 1982: no trainloads of commuters pouring out of it and crossing at the traffic lights, to be dispersed by the gales down Collins Street. The station's row of nine clocks, above its Waterloo-style steps, indicated no departure times on the various routes. Melbourne was the setting for the climax of Nevil Shute's *On The Beach*, but in fact the ending of the world was not about to occur. Instead, the world and his Sheila were heading for the MCG, the Melbourne Cricket Ground.

The MCG is hemmed in by two-tier concrete stands around one half of the arena, and three-tier stands on the other. For a Billy Graham concert this stadium once held 130,000, some sitting on the grass, and 121,000 for a Victorian Football League final.

Seventy-five to eighty thousand spectators entered the ground that day, far more than had been anticipated even for a decisive Test match. Confusion reigned as cars piled up around East Melbourne; too few officials were on duty and they couldn't stop some people getting in free through the turnstiles, let alone prevent them from taking in illegal amounts of liquor in their 'eskies'. It might have comforted the ground administration to know that the scene on January 1, 1862, had been pretty similar, when the first cricket match of its kind was held in Australia between an English team and 'the Colonials' or 'Cornstalks'.

Like other sports brought out by the First Fleet – horse racing, boxing – cricket was closely associated with gambling, and it remained a rollicking, loud, drunken exercise in speculation until Victorian *mores* cleaned it up. But that had not yet happened in Australia when the first English team arrived in 1862 after a ten-week voyage. Roads to the MCG were choked with carriages, buggies and bullock wagons; shooting galleries and hurdy-gurdies competed with the publicans massed under one stand; a passenger balloon was unleashed into the air when the game was over, along with thousands of torn-up betting slips. For this cricket match was one of the great social occasions of the year and the promoters, or in modern parlance the sponsors, were as keen to make capital out of it as any of today's advertising agencies.

These promoters, the catering firm of Spiers and Pond, had originally planned a lecture and reading tour by Charles Dickens, but he did not reply to their invitation. So they dispatched an agent to England, who signed up twelve of the best cricketers of the day to undertake what had not been attempted before: a tour of Australia. A cricket tour to France had been planned as early as 1789, to be cancelled because of faint political rumblings; but this was only the second tour to take place, the first having been by English players to America in 1859. Ten thousand welcomers were on the wharf in Melbourne to cheer ashore these representatives of the Mother Country, who were doubtless the more popular in egalitarian Aussie for being professional cricketers, not socially élite amateurs. They were thence conducted by horse-drawn carriage to Bourke Street and the Café de Paris, owned by Messrs Spiers and Pond.

Their successors, the thirty-fifth English cricket team to visit Australia, under the captaincy of Bob Willis, stayed in the Hilton Hotel just across the road fom the MCG. After breakfast each day the players could thus stroll over to the ground, smelling the camphor from the gum trees – if the strung condition of their nerves allowed them to notice such delights. For Australia were leading in this five-match series, after winning two and drawing the other of the first three Tests: therefore to square it, and retain the semi-mythical prize of the Ashes, England had to win both this match and the last.

Australia has always held a slight edge in cricket, even when England's population was ten times greater. As in other Australian sports the advantages of climate, fine facilities and a highly competitive system based on the metropolis of each state, starting at school level, seem to have insured that whatever talent appears isn't wasted. Overall, Australia by the start of this series had won ninety-three Test Matches, against England's eighty-two, with seventy-two drawn; and that disparity had been further increased during this current tour by two more Australian victories as a result of their finding the extremely fast bowling combination of Rodney Hogg, Geoff Lawson and Jeff Thomson. Hogg had had to move from his native Melbourne to Adelaide before he was recognised, although ockerish at times, as being classical in his method when mind and body clicked; Lawson, lean and Scandinavian-looking, could perhaps deliver the ball even faster; so could

Thomson, a sensation on his first appearance, easy-going only until he took a cricket ball in his hand: then he propelled it as quickly as anyone can ever have done.

In front of a huge crowd in festive mood this triumvirate rapidly resumed from where they had left off in the Brisbane and Adelaide Tests. They took two English wickets before lunch, each celebrated with 10,000 dips into an esky, and a third wicket straight afterwards. Not until Allan Lamb joined Chris Tavaré were England anything but lamb-like, and Tavaré had already been batting over two hours to score a mere twenty-two runs. Then Bruce Yardley bounced in, the burnt-brown West Australian known affectionately as 'Roo', and Tavaré hit him five times to the far corners of the MCG in the space of eight balls. For the first time in this series the Australians were thrown back on their heels: even Bay 13, where *vox populi* sits, went quiet while Lamb and Tavaré pressed on at five runs an over. But when both were dismissed after tea, only Ian Botham of the remaining batsmen could respond to Australian aggression and England's first innings total was no more than 284.

Not quite so many people pushed through the turnstiles on the second morning, but the cricket was no less absorbing, even tense at times, and one moment was electric when Australia's proud Captain, Gregory Chappell, was dismissed by the first ball he received from a twenty-one-year-old Jamaican immigrant playing for England, Norman Cowans.

Negroes have never been allowed into Australia in any numbers. Probably far and away the largest influx came with the American Army, building the road up from Alice Springs in the Second World War, and they did not stay. Negroes were the last people White Australia was going to allow in – yet the most popular, certainly the most applauded, England cricketer on this tour was Cowans. The crowds were manifestly not prejudiced against his colour: what they were concerned about was that Cowans should be given a 'fair go'. Until this Melbourne Test he wasn't. He was the underdog not given a chance – which in cricket terms meant he was not given much bowling to do, and then with an old ball – and Australians rallied to support him as tradition suggested they might.

It was one of the great dethronements. Tall, erect, aloof, for all the world an English Guards officer, Chappell had marched out to bat on this second morning. The rolled-down sleeves of his shirt clung closely; he cast a mere glance at the pitch beneath him. He wore no protective helmet as lesser batsmen did; but naturally he would play the hook stroke from in front of his face if Cowans dared to pitch one short at him. He had done so on the last occasion he had confronted Cowans – had hooked him and been caught on the boundary at Brisbane by Lamb. So England's captain again sent Lamb out to deep square-leg, in front of the massive video scoreboard and a huge distance from the wicket. Chappell deigned to notice, assumed his stance in the crease. Cowans began his lengthy run, accelerated, leapt and served a bouncer at Chappell for his first ball. To leave it alone would have been a point to Cowans and an affront to himself, so Chappell hooked, and middled the ball, cracked it a long way, perhaps ninety yards. But just inside the boundary fence, ninety-one yards away, was Lamb who scarcely had to move before he received the ball like a baseball outfielder. Then the South African-born Lamb and the West Indian-born Cowans raced to congratulate each other in the Caribbean fashion, by raising both hands and slapping the other's up-turned palms.

While eleven England players celebrated, 53,000 Australians watched silently. Chappell marched stiffly back; the video screen replayed his fatal stroke. Australia had lost two wickets for very few runs, then a third wicket, and a fourth when Botham bowled the out-of-form Allan Border straight after lunch: Australia were having the worst of it for the first time in this series. The match and tempers smouldered further when Botham appealed vehemently to the umpire for a leg-before decision against the vice-captain, Kim Hughes, and the blond superstar, David Hookes. When these appeals were rejected, Botham's outbursts of disgust were replayed on the vast video, to mass derision.

Hughes and Hookes both went on to score half-centuries;

so did Rodney Marsh. But England persevered through late afternoon to dismiss Australia for 287 in their first innings. On top of a drought such as Melbourne had rarely known, the evening humidity, unrelieved by any wind, had turned the players' hair to mats of sweat. The torrid day finally over, the players walked limply home through camphorous leaves around the park, mixing democratically with the masses flooding out of the biggest cricket ground in the world.

Lygon Street, where the famous rows of restaurants are, is an area of black hair and moustaches; part of the eastern Mediterranean; a reminder that one in every four Australians is a product of immigration from a non-English-speaking country. What francophone Montreal is to Paris, Melbourne is to Athens – the city with the second largest number of Greek speakers. In Lygon Street there's a Greek pharmacy every few hundred yards, advertising in its windows the next Neil Sedaka concert. Lebanese cafés serve black aromatic coffee in small cups, and offer a range of nuts, especially pistachios, for the discerning Near Eastern palate. A pizzeria waits for the first of the night's take-aways: no smell of crisp pizzas yet but of lunchtime's greasy chips, while its jukebox thumps out the latest Demis Roussos.

Out of a Turkish café on the corner came the mighty rushing wind of an espresso machine: inside, a few dark figures clustered round a week-old edition of *Hurriyet*. Next door was a Lebanese 'Bring-Your-Own-Alcohol' restaurant: the owner's daughters were plying pitta bread around a plate of hummus, his sons working behind the counter. Maronite Christians. Dad came to Australia in the mid-seventies, found he could get a work permit, phoned home to Beirut and told his family to follow. 'Is the war,' he says. 'Is very bad in Beirut, believe me.'

After the Second World War Australia's preferred order of immigrants was first the British, then Northern Europeans (Dutch and Germans in particular, being the least 'different'), then Eastern Europeans (including all the various Yugoslavs), followed by Southern Europeans – Greeks,

Italians, Maltese. The more favoured immigrants received assisted passages. By the time it came to Turks and Greeks and Lebanese, who were less likely to be skilled workers, the majority had to pay their own fares.

The owner of another pharmacy in Lygon Street said he had seen an advertisement back in his native village in Greece in the fifties, and had applied to the Australian consulate for a permit. He was one of the lucky minority: got an assisted passage, paid five pounds towards his berth. Within a week of arrival he had found first one job and then a second with the enthusiasm of most migrants, and his family followed him out in ones and twos as he sent home his savings. He had married a Greek wife, naturally – statistics say that the British, North Americans and Dutch are the most likely migrants to marry native Australians – but he was becoming ever more Australianised: thus he had been 'a-watching the Test match on TV and Dennis Lillee, why he no playing? Dennis Lillee, he a great player.'

The federal government's policy used to be 'assimilation' – everyone to be Aussie. Now the catchphrase has changed to 'integration' – national groups to maintain their cultural identity inside the one great melting-pot. Cuisine is always given as the stock example: these Greek and Italian restaurants in Lygon Street are patronised by everyone, not just by Greeks and Italians – so Australia's world of food is full of diversity, a meritocracy, with excellence the only criterion. And this ideal state *has* been attained: one afternoon in Sydney a digger came into a milk bar, a real digger who was working on the road outside with a power drill and dressed in no more than shorts and boots. In a dinky-di accent he ordered the drinks required to quench the thirst of himself and his mate: two *capuccinos. Capuccinos!* The old steak-and-eggs Aussie has had his eyes and mouth opened by Mediterraneans first, then Chinese, Thais, Indians and the rest.

But is food the exception? Is there an intermingling of culture as well as cuisine? Most commentators say not yet. There are Greek Australian poets who are famous back in Salonika, but no one in Wagga Wagga has heard of them:

as far as anyone there is concerned the Greek cultural contribution is *souvlaki*. 'Ethnic TV', as the foreign language channel is known, may typify the present degree of integration in Australia. Non-English-language films stay on that channel and are never shown by the mass commercial stations. 'Ethnic' and 'Aussie' may be in the same melting-pot, but they're still a bit oil-and-waterish.

Early days though: the children of post-war immigrants have barely grown up. Some of them, like the Yugoslavs and Chinese, will take longer to integrate than others but it seems they will all come together eventually – and, outside the restaurants, probably in the sporting community before anywhere else. Soccer has expanded as rapidly as it has because it is the game familiar to European migrants, and therefore everyone can understand it. But even the incomprehensible game of cricket is starting to appeal now to the Greek pharmacist, relaxing in his armchair, while his sons have been playing it at school for years.

After the Test matches were over, England beat Australia in one of a series of limited-overs matches in Adelaide. I happened to be in the home of a Dutch friend when his ten-year-old daughter came home distraught, for she had been to the Adelaide Oval and seen Australia beaten. When she saw this Englishman – and she was on the verge of tears and stamping her foot – she vented her wrath by saying: 'We might have lost today – but we're going to kill you in Perth.' 'We', already.

That week the Test cricketers enjoyed no respite. For the third day running they returned to the fray, in effect level-pegging – England only three runs behind after one innings per side. Since a draw was improbable with plenty of time remaining, Australia would either go three-nil up in the series or be reduced to a two-one lead, with one game in Sydney to play.

England lost three of their second innings wickets before lunch. Hogg bowled Tavaré with the same kind of ball, cutting in, that he had dismissed England's master batsman Geoff Boycott with a few years before, thus raising the

MCG's multitude to a feverpitch that Billy Graham might have envied. England rallied a little during the afternoon, until Thomson broke Graeme Fowler's toe and his concentration. England, 129 for five wickets, were dependent upon their waning champion, Botham, in his belligerence more Australian than the Australians.

Even some Australian followers of cricket might have been pleased to see England, as the underdogs, make a recovery hereabouts and win this match, so that purist interest in this series would be maintained to the end of it. But beating the Mother Country has ultimately to be more important still. On the last occasion that England had played a Test match in Melbourne their captain, Mike Brearley, was booed so loudly whenever he entered the arena that Australia's team manager had apologised for the mass uproar. Few if any cricketers can have been booed so loudly and sustainedly since – well, since another England captain had been derided by *vox populi Australis*, D. R. Jardine. Both Brearley and Jardine were known as Oxbridge products, Establishment figures in background if not in substance; but that does not in itself explain why they roused so much hostility in many Australians. I feel there's one possible explanation: that both men, as English captains, evoked, and in their bearing personified, another kind of English captain – those British army officers of the First World War who blew their whistles and sent so many Australians to their deaths at Gallipoli and the Somme. This type of Pom touched a still-raw nerve.

Bay 13 and surrounding stands kept cheering as England sagged to 201 for seven wickets. Botham went, and Geoff Miller; only three wickets left. But rallying again, England reached 294 by the end of the third evening, which meant three astonishingly close, neck-and-neck totals had been recorded and Australia had to score 292 to win.

Thirty-seven thousand arrived on the fourth morning to watch them do it, or fail to do it as seemed more probable when Cowans took the new ball and dethroned Chappell a second time. Chappell tried to put Cowans in his place by whacking him through the covers: England's chirpy Cockney substitute, Ian Gould, dived for the catch. Australia had lost two other wickets for ninety-nine by lunch – advantage to England – but tipped the balance back to equilibrium by reaching 176 for five wickets by tea on another oppressive, sapping afternoon.

Cowans tipped the balance back again to England. Walking slowly to the start of his run-up, breathing deeply, filling the full volume of his Negro chest, he moved into that phase of third or fourth wind when an athlete performs above himself. He dismissed three of Australia's five remaining wickets, and caught the fourth. That should have settled it. Only the last pair of Border and Thomson remained to score the seventy-four remaining runs, something beyond the ability of any last-wicket pair in the history of one thousand Test matches or so played in the previous hundred years.

But England by the end of this fourth evening were enervated. Border and Thomson hit off exactly half of those runs before the close, leaving thirty-seven more to be scored on the fifth and final morning. Now the newspapers did their part: their back pages, and their front, suggested that Australia could do it in the face of all precedent. The words of the old Australian bowler, Spofforth, uttered just before his team beat England on English soil for the first time, were recalled as a rallying cry: 'This thing can be done!' Then another instance of an Australian last-wicket pair knocking off runs to beat West Indies was cited. Any propaganda that might daunt English confidence is legitimate!

And to daunt the Poms still further, Melburnians flood boldly through the turnstiles as ten-thirty approaches, although they may in fact have travelled miles to see one minute of action, or less, should England dismiss that final wicket at the outset. But England don't, and spectators continue pouring into the MCG until 18,000 are officially estimated to be present. Sydney-siders will argue that the crowd was so large because there's nothing else to do in Melbourne, but even in busy Sydney a number growing into millions must have been turning on television and radio as Australia edged nearer to their target. Not to forget those in the Ironclad at Marble Bar, in Alice Springs and

Pine Creek, in Zeehan and Far North Queensland, for whom cricket – as the only major team-sport played in every state – is one of the unifying elements bringing the nation together, like the Melbourne Cup and Anzac Day.

At first the huge stadium is hushed – after all, Australia's case is scarcely better than hopeless. But as Border and Thomson survive England's opening assault and they begin to score the occasional single, the crowd cautiously finds its voice. Inter-state rivalry counts for nothing now: never mind that Border and Thomson were both from New South Wales originally and had moved on to Queensland, so long as the Poms are beaten. 'Bord-er! Bord-er!' – the sound reverberated around the concrete stands as the little fox-terrier of a left-hander drove and cut and brought sweat to the backs of Englishmen, though the morning was cloudy and relatively cool.

During the first six overs – each survived ball of each over being greeted with relief – the scoreboard as well as time almost stands still. Four runs are added; England take the new ball; the action moves forward towards its climax. The English players apparently give themselves over to fate. Willis, their captain, puts his head down, runs in to bowl and keeps 'plugging away', as he summarised his approach afterwards. But the Australians know what they are doing, what they want out of life; their survival instinct is not in doubt.

Runs come in singles only until the morning's ninth over, when Border is able to steal two runs because all England's fielders are guarding the boundary to prevent fours. At that point, Australia 266 or twenty-six runs away, Willis bowls to Thomson and the whole crowd gasps in horror when the video replay shows Thomson had carved the ball off his middle stump, straight to cover. Naught abashed 'Thommo' tries it again and carves three runs past cover: he is the bleach-haired 'surfie', spontaneous, content with life on a fishing-boat and the beach, instinctive. Off the last ball of this over Border pushes a single, Thomson starts late, and two England fielders scramble for the ball, knocking themselves over in the process while he makes his ground.

The first signs of panic by England; Australia are twenty-two runs from home.

In the morning's eleventh over Border pushes two more runs to reach his own half-century and the MCG resounds with its tremendous shout of 'Border! Border!' But then this 'barracking' – supporting, not denigrating – originated in Australia, in Sydney during the 1840s. When the old race-course was turned into the colony's main cricket ground, right beside it was a pub, on the corner of what are now Park and Elizabeth Streets. To encourage custom, the publican offered free drinks for every batsman who struck a ball over a nearby row of oak trees. This combination of gambling and grog increased his turnover at the same time as encouraging his regular customers to establish the Australian tradition of being cricket's greatest barrackers.

Drinks are brought out, soft ones, after Border has gathered in eight more runs in ones and scurried twos. He is helped by England's tactics of dispersing their fielders and making no attempt to catch him out. As the English players drain their glasses, with only fourteen runs to go, they can see themselves losing this game, and the series.

But Botham is bowling now, which means that England's self-conviction hasn't quite ebbed away. Yet he is not the bowler he was: Thomson carves rather than cuts him for two runs, then almost for a priceless four, except that Gould at cover-point stops the ball with his shins. Thomson next takes a single, as does Border off Willis – ten to win.

That target is brought down to single figures, then to a mere six runs when Border leans into a full-length ball from Botham and sends it through the English cover field. David Gower sprints in pursuit while the batsmen are borne between wickets as much by the crowd's noise and passion as by their legs. 'Border! Border!' resounds in waves from the cavernous stands of the MCG. At this point Australia have become favourites to win: Border and Thomson have turned outside hopes into an expectation of victory, which puts the onus upon them. Clearly the sponsors (Benson and Hedges now, not Spiers and Pond) expect victory too, for they announce that gold medallions will be struck in honour of this last-ditch pair, if – tempting fate – they bring it off.

Border glances two more runs off Willis – only four to go. England's captain, though he doesn't know it, is bowling his last over of the match. He looks to be at the end of his tether as well, sombre-eyed and hollow-cheeked, rare flickers of expression crossing his face. Botham takes the ball; he hasn't lost hope. He runs in at Thomson who, now aware of the enormity of his imminent achievement, decides to play in a textbook manner instead of spontaneously unleashing one of his unorthodox cuts or carves. As a result he merely pushes his bat at the ball, which flies off the outside edge towards Tavaré, who sees it all the way against the background of Bay 13, but when he brings his hands up to his chest the ball bounces out and upwards over his head, where it hangs, and England's last chance with it – until it begins its descent, when Miller dashes across from first slip, stoops towards his shins and clutches it less than a foot from the ground.

Thomson is out. Australia have lost. The MCG at first doesn't quite know what to do. They watch silently as the England players leap and congratulate each other. But soon they seem to decide that though it is a defeat, it is so valiant a defeat – by only three runs, equalling the narrowest-ever margin in Test cricket – that Border and Thomson are heroes after all, up there in the sporting pantheon with Rod Laver and Herb Elliot, John Newcombe, and the whole yachting team of Australia II which took the America's Cup.

Sport brings the nation together – even Melbourne's Greeks will be proud of 'their' cricketers, especially as they go on to win the Ashes. And if sport plays what may strike some as an unduly large role in the nation's life, then in part it is filling a vacuum by giving the country a national sense which other, older societies may take for granted.

7
Melbourne to Sydney

'Think of the paralysis of intellect that gave that idea birth.'
(Mark Twain, upon the diversity of gauges in Australia)

Until 1930, Melbourne and Adelaide were the only state capitals one could travel between without having to change trains. They shared a five-foot-three-inch gauge. This is slightly ironical, as it might be remarked that while they shared broadness of gauge they did not then share broadness of mind, being the centres of Wowserism. This may possibly derive from We Only Want Social Evils Remedied (or Rectified) but certainly defines that rigidly censorious, puritan, blue-stocking attitude which was so influential in Australia until only a generation ago.

The pleasure of changing trains, and gauges, usually occurred in the middle of the night and it was such an inconvenience on the Melbourne to Sydney run which prompted Twain's outburst. Before Federation this annoyance was aggravated when, having dressed and stumbled into the night, crossing from station to station by horse-drawn coach, a passenger had also to escort his baggage through customs. At the state border on the banks of the Murray River, cases had to be examined and duty paid, unless they were put in the guard's van and consigned straight through to their destination, to be inspected there. 'Is this a trimmed bonnet, madam?' a customs officer would have enquired. 'In that case it will be dutiable. Is that harmonium of yours new, sir? If so, duty will have to be paid I'm afraid, but not if it's an old one.' Victoria, strong in manufacturing, was even more protectionist than mercantilist and pastoral New South Wales: Victoria had 333 categories of dutiable goods.

It was something of a triumph, therefore, in 1883 to get the two rival colonies so closely connected as to share, if not gauges, then at least the same station on their border. In that year, a proper inter-capital service began, doing the 576 miles in twenty and a half hours and beginning like most inaugurations on Australian railways with an enormous banquet. The Marquis of Normanby, Governor of Victoria, was present at these celebrations to say that he believed 'the inevitable result of railway union will ultimately be the larger union of the Colonies themselves'. After eighteen more years of rivalry and going through customs in the middle of the night, his prophecy about union came true with Federation, but the total unification of the Victorian and New South Wales gauges did not follow until 1962 when the Southern Aurora first ran.

Five years before then, in 1957, it had finally been decided that standardisation of gauges between Perth, Sydney, Melbourne and Brisbane had to be achieved in spite of the enormous cost involved. 'Unification of railway gauges may decide whether we hold our country,' warned Sir Harold Clapp in the Gauge Standardisation Report of 1948. 'During the last war it took thirty-five days to shift a division from Sydney to Perth, and then it arrived without its guns. With standard gauge it would take eight days. There are still people in high places who oppose rail unification. It is true and incredible.'

This confusion, not unpredictably, is traceable to Celtic origins. Until an Irishman called Shields came along, everything was plain steaming: the Gauge Act had been passed in the United Kingdom in 1846 and Gladstone, as Secretary of State for War and the Colonies, had recommended Australians to employ the British four feet eight and a half inches. But Shields believed the Irish gauge of five feet three inches to be superior and convinced the directors of the Sydney Railway Company of as much. They in turn persuaded the Colonial Secretary to agree, and in 1852 an Act was passed to legislate for a five-feet-three-inch broad gauge in New South Wales. Victoria and South Australia, not having embarked on any railways yet themselves, sensibly agreed to follow suit and all was well.

Shields, however, resigned and was succeeded as Chief Engineer of the Sydney Railway Company by an equally vehement and uncompromising Scotsman called Wallace. He insisted on the British standard gauge for New South Wales and had the 1852 Act repealed. The other two states were furious, naturally so since they had by now ordered their broad-gauge rolling stock. They refused to back down and went their own way; Victoria, internally, still is broad-gauged; Queensland and Western Australia, when they came to build their systems, chose the cheaper narrow gauge; Tasmania opted for both broad and narrow, not to mention some ultra-narrow gauge lines as well. This 'paralysis of intellect', born of obstinacy, lasted over a century.

Now nothing is particularly notable on the overnight journey from Melbourne. You go aboard one evening and wake up next morning to tea, biscuits and the outskirts of Sydney. There's no changing trains in the freezing cold at Albury-Wodonga, no customs officers and dutiable bonnets, just an ample dinner. It's all efficient, punctual (well, fairly) and standardised. To see something of the countryside between Australia's two great cities, including its capital, one has to make a few digressions.

The long-standing jibe about Canberra is that it has no soul. It's an easy jibe, one that could be levelled just as readily at other instant, purpose-built capitals like Brasilia or Islamabad. But Manning Clark, the historian, sitting in his bush hat and Canberra garden, will have none of it: he believes that a soul is growing, along with the trees.

Pretty barren at the time of its foundation, Canberra was at first planted with European trees on the same cultural-cringe principle that impelled members of the Adelaide Club never to stock Australian wines until 1946. Not until the 1960s were native trees reckoned to be fit for the nation's capital. Today there's a mixture, and in the autumn when the frosts are crisp at 2,500 feet, the deciduous shedding their leaves against a backcloth of gums makes a combination that is the best of European and Antipodean.

However, while it may be conceded that the city is developing a soul, it must still be open to question whether it has a heart. There are no 'have-nots' living in Canberra: they were long ago shunted into Queanbeyan, the next town down, and their weatherboard houses demolished. Then years of Menzies and Malcolm Fraser did nothing to disturb the growth of a sense of complacency among the bureaucrats. Canberra was encouraged to become heartless, being so remote from the nation's life, from unemployment and the realities of under-privilege – everyone in Canberra seems to earn more than the national average and to drive around on an expense account; and remote in a sense from the cares of international life as well, Canberra – perhaps symbolically – being the only capital in Australia that is inland and without an international airport.

The writer John Gunther, when he finally got round to including Australia in his 'Inside' series, set out to discover 'who runs Australia?' But he died (of natural causes, beyond suspicion) before he arrived at any conclusion. Is the power centre in Canberra, the political capital? Or Sydney, the largest city? Or Melbourne, the financial capital and seat of the Melbourne Club? (News item: 'Melbourne. From our Staff Representative – Seventeen unemployed people were arrested after invading the exclusive Melbourne Club yesterday. The group's spokeswoman, Colleen Hartland, said: "We are trying to highlight the plight of the unemployed who have no money or food. The real politics of this country goes on in places like the Melbourne Club. This is where decisions are made, not in Parliament."')

The existence of strong, all-but-autonomous states was one consideration which led Gunther to think there was no single all-pervading power group. And that appears still to be true, although there is an increasing and disturbing tendency for more and more monopolies to become concentrated in fewer and fewer hands, for example in the media, where the Fairfax, Murdoch and Packer groups have come to hold every card. Donald Horne agrees with Gunther: 'To suggest that in Australian society there is a self-perpetuating and ideologically cohesive class that monopolises privilege is simply ridiculous.'

Thus Australia can happily claim not to be dominated by those traditional social élites which, in England, continue to pack Eton, Winchester, Oxbridge, and to retain much of their influence. Australia, obviously, had a power vacuum in 1788 and it has been impossible for any one group to become entrenched everywhere and to take hold of all the strings. Yet, far less happily, this absence of a traditional establishment has meant that many power-hungry groups have been able to seize some of the strings for themselves and some pretty undesirable groups have done so, especially in the field of organised crime. It seems, in fact, that Australia has an underworld on the American or Italian scale, not restricted by strong centralised law enforcement as in Western Europe. The numbers of members of the Painters and Dockers Union who suddenly disappear in front of a crowd of witnesses – who, inexplicably, are never able to remember anything about the event afterwards – would do credit to any Mafiosi. If you keep your nose clean, of course, as an ordinary member of the public, you'll be all right. But the underworld in some cities is coming terrifyingly close to emerging into broad daylight, as was recently emphasised by two Royal Commissions of Enquiry, which declared that the threat from organised crime would be the greatest challenge to Australian public life in the 1980s.

From Canberra a far better way to Sydney than the brisk overnight ride is the leisurely train down through the Blue Mountains. In Lithgow, there is the diversion of steam engines puffing up the preserved section of the famous Lithgow Link; and Katoomba has what is claimed to be the steepest railway in the world. It plunges down a bushy hillside with a gradient, at its steepest and queasiest, of fifty-two degrees. Happily, it may also be the briefest of rail journeys, since it takes only a couple of minutes to do the 230 metres in two little wire-covered cages. Should the ascent make you feel like a sack of coal being pulled up a mine shaft, that was the original idea. For this cable railway was built in the 1890s to haul up coal and shale deposited in the valley more than 200 million years before, when the Blue Mountains were lapped by sea. This line, and an aerial ropeway that soon broke (leaving the hillside strewn with skips) transported the coal from the valley floor to Katoomba, thence to Sydney. New South Wales is still the largest black coal-producing state, but without any output nowadays from Katoomba's mines.

Tourism was quick to supercede coal. The Blue Mountain air was reckoned to be so invigorating, the situation of Katoomba so convenient and panoramic, that by the turn of this century a week's sojourn there became quite the fashion amongst the beaux and belles of Sydney society. It was also a convenient place to pursue discrete *amours*, in hotels where it was the practice to ring a bell in the corridors an hour before dawn so that gentlemen might return to their rooms and maintain appearances. The Governor of New South Wales from 1885 to 1890 lent his patronage to this flourishing resort and allowed the most respectable of these hotels to be named after him. A minute's walk from the station, the Carrington in a way is as remarkable now as ever it was in its *belle-époque* heyday.

Brighton and Cheltenham boast numerous such decaying piles, damply bankrupt victims of spiralling labour costs and excessive heating bills. The Carrington, however, staggers on, if only with the momentum of a drunkard keeling over. Its peeling paint and need for refurbishing are hidden by a brave array of log fires, black and gold wallpaper and noticeboards displaying the annual winners of the Carrington Ladies Bowls Cup. Waitresses flounce about the chandeliered dining-room in white pastry-cook caps and adeptly dangle a provocative ringlet against one's cheek as they dish from the silver tureen of consommé. Guests are not only fashionable beaux up from Sydney: that hearty laughter from the table over there comes from the fleshy jowls of the Rotarians at their monthly dinner. But if the atmosphere is cheap and cheerful, the décor fading and garish, the jollity at least is genuine; it is not the forced gaiety of an English Christmas, but spontaneous *joie de vivre*, egged on by the scrapings of the resident string trio. Australians celebrate well: unlike the English they need no war to remind them to live for the moment.

Always has the Carrington's popularity been intimately linked with the fortunes of the railway up from Sydney. When the latter was electrified, after the Second World War, a trip to the Blue Mountains lost some of its appeal as an adventure. Now the prospect is that its Greek owner will turn the Carrington into a money-spinning casino to make ends meet. So the place will have to play its own roulette: gamble or die.

From Katoomba, at a height of over 3,300 feet, the line descends all the way to the plains. The one date every Australian schoolchild knows after Botany Bay is the Crossing of the Blue Mountains in 1813: and the route taken by Blaxland, Wentworth and Lieutenant Lawson did not stray far from that of the later rail track. It was the white man's first penetration of the Great Dividing Range which, for the first twenty-five years of white settlement, had lived up to its name by keeping out explorers. Then with Gregory Blaxland as leader, a moustachioed free settler eager to find fresh grazing land at a time of drought, an expedition set out accompanied by four servants and four pack animals. It took them eighteen days of following the watershed to find a path to the top, whereupon 'their provisions exhausted, they returned to civilisation'. Appropriately, these explorers are now immortalised in the names of the stations down from Katoomba, though it was more than half a century before Wascoe's station was changed to Blaxland, Blue Mountains to Lawson, and Weatherboard to Wentworth Falls.

These are Swiss Alpine stations, neat and wooden. The train – of double-decker carriages – winds through them at less than forty miles an hour, since the track is so steep and twisting. Gums cover the whole of the hills, endless seeming, on the surface unvarying; yet there is a variety nevertheless amongst these interminable gums. Some are blackened by fire, others are pale ghost gums. Young ones reach straight for the sunlight; older gums, having attained it, relapse into curvature of the spine. It is their eucalyptus oil, mixing with dust, which is said to make these mountains blue (whereas in Jamaica's Blue Mountains, it is the richness of the foliage, heightened by the evening light). These eucalypts are accompanied by the odd turpentine tree or the yellowness of wattle.

Blaxland had set out from his farm near Emu Plains, where the Blue Mountains finally come to earth. From there, today's train passes through almost continuous ribbon development until it arrives in the centre of Sydney. The bungalows begin, of tile, brick and board; the neon 'M' of the first McDonalds hove into sight. In sheer acreage, Los Angeles is the biggest city on earth, but Australian cities, having the very low average density of sixteen people per residential acre, sprawl more than most. Sydney can seem as vast as L.A. if you approach it from the west because, with nothing to the east but ocean, Sydney elongates westward, reproducing suburb after suburb, like amoeba made up of wires and drains and bungalows and aerials, all but identical, with fence and drive and washing line.

From Sydney's westernmost fringe – and it will soon be a megalopolis right up to Emu Plains – the distance to the centre is thirty-five kilometres. Do it by car and you stop at every traffic light on the Parramatta Road. Bunting streams over 'used car' plazas ('pre-owned' is the latest euphemism). Hotels are executives' accommodation units, each with its shower, kettle and 'individual' milk containers, insufficient for even one serving. The expansive Carrington is more than two hours away, more like an age.

Through this pre-fabbery the silver train glides, sleek as a French loaf in foil. Its air-conditioning whispers, tinted windows insulate it from the world outside. Though the rush is inaudible, out there it is rush hour: commuters are on the move again. Cars wait, fuming at traffic lights: stopping trains pick up and slowly set down. For in Australia, because of this low density of population, commuting is over greater distances – and therefore takes longer – than anywhere in the West.

Time budget studies are recent in Australia, as in most

countries. But sufficient research has been done to present a reliable picture, which in turn can be contrasted with the data amassed in Alexander Szalai's study of 1972 that was based on a selection of cities in twelve countries. In none of the countries studied was the amount of time spent in commuting anything like as long as in Australia. The average for weekday commuting (to work and back) ranged from sixteen minutes in some super-efficient West German city, up to forty-one minutes in a number of Bulgarian and Hungarian cities. The contrast is remarkable with Australia's two largest: in Melbourne, the average weekday journey time, according to a 1975 study, is sixty-three minutes, and in Sydney, one hour (the 'average resident' of both cities being employed nine kilometres from his home). Their citizens therefore spend four times as long in commuting as good German burghers, roughly twice as long as most of their western counterparts, and half as long again as members of the Communist bloc. Australians have not been widely recognised for what they are: the western world's most enthusiastic commuters.

Australian sociologists have concluded that this commuting is undertaken voluntarily. 'An individual considering where to live balances his distaste for the journey to work against his demand for a pleasant home and his ability to pay for it,' the theory goes. Nevertheless, the question remains to be answered; is it really a good bargain – so many hours of an individual's life spent commuting in return for a 'better' home?

A city dominated by a functional waterway has the advantage of a natural heart, and even Trollope upon seeing Sydney Harbour admitted himself unable to extol its wonders properly.

Sydney Harbour is not merely sailed and wind-surfed upon; it is used by ferries and hydrofoils to transport Sydneysiders in the course of their daily living, and also by naval ships and submarines, by ocean liners and oil tankers. Perhaps it is not quite so teeming with workaday purpose as the Golden Horn, for instance, where Istanbulis eat, sleep and make a living on or out of the water; but the

Harbour is integral nonetheless, being far more than the ornament which the river Yarra is to Melbourne or the Thames is becoming to London or the Seine to Paris.

And King's Cross on a hill above the Harbour is Sydney's Soho; the old Swan-and-Edgar principle applies here, if slightly revised, that sooner or later you'll meet everyone you'd rather not know. For one does see all sorts at the Cross: like a Lesbian couple I saw walking down the main boulevard of Darlinghurst Street one evening. One of them, presumably 'active', could have been a mud-wrestler, being my height of six foot three or four, considerably more stocky, and dressed in a boiler suit – 'passive' more demurely. Going the opposite way down the pavement were a normal-looking heterosexual couple, the middle-aged wife well dressed-up and sporting a careful hair-do. She bumped into 'passive', who momentarily reeled back. Whereupon, 'active' roared at the wife: 'Watch which way you're bloody going – SLUT!!!'

The mid- and late-sixties were the Cross's great days of R and R. American servicemen might not have appreciated Melbourne quite so much for Rest and Recreation during their break from Vietnam, but they loved Sydney, so that a King's Cross waitress could pick up four hundred dollars a week in tips alone and a taxi driver as much as a thousand dollars, especially if he took his passengers to the adjoining suburb by way of the airport. Steak bars and pros opened their arms to GI's; the streets flowed with bourbon and Jack Daniels. After the Second World War, the Cross had settled down into being a quiet backwater for Hungarian immigrants, but 'Nam spurred it into big business and racketeering. The gays flooded in to offer their services to the Services. Few remain though: Oxford Street is now their sphere of influence and around the Cross you no longer run the risk of bumping into a sixteen-stone Maori drag queen.

Dull eyes, doped to withstand the evening's work, take some sparkle out of the bright lights, as does the rubbish – the most profuse refuse in a litter-conscious country. But King's Cross is too busy having itself a good time to worry about finer details. There's indulgence to be

131

had in a back-street hotel for half an hour, or a strip show at 'Les Girls' or in the 'adult book stores'; there are tacos, crêpes, shawarmas, salads and gelati in addition to pimps, fixers, bouncers and heavies; piccolo bars and pizzerias as well as degradation and bondage. In these activities the migrants tend to play a full part, not only in the restaurants of their various national cuisines: Maoris and Maltese are often the bouncers, the pimps Greek, Lebanese or Hungarian. Native Australians are said to fill the niches at both the bottom (pros and mud-wrestlers) and the top (Abe, The Boss), paying off the police and politicians.

'Sydney has always been a rough-edged, dynamic, cosmopolitan city,' was Maximilian Walsh's summary in *Poor Little Rich Country*, '. . . while Melbourne with its temperate climate has had a more structured society, which has been more concerned with cerebral and intellectual pursuits than the people of Sydney, whose interests centre on physical activities.' Melbourne was the stronghold of figurative painting; Sydney of abstract expressionism. Melbourne dines out in BYOs, Sydney prefers a night out 'on the Cross' or heads for one of the 1,600 Leagues Clubs which are a speciality of New South Wales – more likely the latter, because the Cross is for the affluent and foreigners, while these de-luxe versions of the north of England working men's club are for the majority.

Down Anzac Parade a typical club – big, but not the biggest – advertises in neon the forthcoming attraction of *Las Vegas By Night*. But this evening patrons have to be content with *Caligula* at eight p.m. and of course with the poker machines. Classical statues lead us to them along the corridors of this pleasure dome, a cathedral erected to the greater glory of gambling.

On the Ghan up to Alice Springs, I'd heard a retired couple mention this club and its 'beautiful facilities': lounge bars, restaurants, snooker tables, a dance hall, poker-machine areas, all of them decorated in a most arresting colour scheme. Whatever was not lilac, or green, or red, was a bright mauve, or as Barry Humphries would pronounce it, 'mauvé'. Upstairs, on the mezzanine floor, some shelves had been set aside for the Club library; and literature had been divided up under the headings of Large Novels, Paperbacks, Mills & Boone, Crime, Westerns, Georgette Heyer and – to lend variety – Light Romance.

All these beautiful facilities are subsidised by the 'pokies', rows and rows of fruit machines. By seven in the evening, only half of the several hundred machines were having their arms pulled, but by nine o'clock all were taken (at weekends, queues will form behind the 'lucky' pokies, though how any of them can be thought lucky is a mystery, since they are all programmed to return no more than eighty to eighty-five per cent of the money placed in them).

I went up to a kiosk where a young lady in orange changed my two dollars into ten-cent pieces: they barely covered the bottom of my paper coin cup. Many patrons, however, held cups that were filled to the brim or had more than one cup. Eventually, a machine fell free – a ten center, considered to be inferior to the more aristocratic twenty-cent machines – and I installed myself on a stool in front of one which called itself 'Random Harvest' and purported to make payments of up to 200 coins for various winning combinations and 5,000 for the jackpot – 'All pays in coins'. Given this inducement, I put my coins in one by one, yanked at the handle as everyone else in my row was doing, like a line of battery chickens pecking at seed, then waited for my seed to bear fruit while lights flashed and the wheels went ding-a-ding-ding. Nothing happened. Twenty coins – a round score – went into that machine and not one ever manifested itself again. I would agree that I was harvested, but personally and comprehensively, not in the least randomly.

Turning to my right to find someone with whom I could air my grievances, a tender scene presented itself: man and wife together, beside a machine. Love is pulling your partner's handle while she concentrates on the pay-outs. 'Touch of Gold' was their machine's name, yet although Midas himself could not influence the outcome, that doesn't stop 1,700 million dollars being invested annually in the pokies of New South Wales.

Research reveals that many patrons have their favourite

machine and jealously guard it: an ashtray placed in the pay-out tray is the accepted sign that a pokey is reserved. Those that play a nice bleepy tune with each pay-out are especially popular. But aficionados are found to tire of a machine after two or three years, so that it has to be replaced with a new one which has a bleepier tune or a more exotic title: thus Easy Street, Raindrops and Random Harvest give way to Aristocrat Trumps, Touch of Gold and Inca Royal.

This club, with several hundred pokies (costing six thousand dollars each), is one of half a dozen in New South Wales to make an annual profit over two million dollars – some of that profit going to finance the club's rugby league team. That is after licences and taxes have been paid to the state government: by charging two hundred dollars licence fee for every ten-cent machine, more for the twenty-centers, and by supplementary taxes on club profits, the New South Wales Treasury rakes in around one hundred and fifty million dollars a year through the pokies. No wonder it thinks they're a good thing. But New South Wales is the only state that has legalised them so far.

It's all part of that legendary love of a flutter – one Australian legend that has a basis in modern fact. International statistics are pretty useless for comparison because they do not include illegal as well as legal gambling, but from the few studies that have been done it has been generally concluded that Australians spend more on gambling per capita than any other people in the world. In New South Wales, the total comes to one-sixth of the net average income – over a thousand dollars per person per year. While pokies are the main form of gambling there, every state has lotteries ('Go Lotto! Go Lotto! You're mad if you don't!') whose winning draws are frequently televised live, in addition to sweepstakes, raffles and bingo, as well as the many forms of racing on which to bet. This partiality for forms of gambling in which no skill is required has been related to the Australian idea of egalitarianism: all are equal when the gambling starts, no one is superior or better qualified than anyone else, the fortune could go anyone's way.

Betting on horse and dog racing attracts equally large sums, either legally through the Totalisator Agency Board and on-course bookmakers, or illegally through off-course bookmakers (of which every pub is said to have one). There must be truth in the suggestion that because every white Australian or his forefathers gambled at some stage in going to Australia, he is therefore going to be well-disposed towards another gamble once he's got there. Another theory is that it's a case of speculation on uncertainty acting as an antidote to the regularity of commuting and suburban existence.

Around the rest of the complex the restaurants were by now in full swing, particularly the Chinese one, where the spring rolls were going down a treat as an entrée, followed by beef and black bean sauce, or sweet and sour pork, or chicken and almonds, rounded off invariably with fried ice cream.

A more basic self-service canteen was situated next to the dance floor so that diners and dancers could together enjoy the three-man band. Greek and Yugoslav women, hair close-cropped, forgot their successful small businesses for a moment and took breathless turns on the floor. Dimitri and his mates from the same Greek village had a go too, undoing the top buttons of their shirts to proclaim they are well enough established now to be on the look-out for a girlfriend. Vietnamese queued at the counter, Indians, Sri Lankans and young men from Hong Kong – it's cheapest to eat at the club and there's plenty of food around in the land of opportunity. Croatian men at the canteen tables, and wives already large – proving there's no exaggeration in the survey figure that over forty per cent of Australian women are obese, and half the men – picked up another whole slice of bread and butter and brought it to their mouths to toast their new prosperity: 'You be right, mate?' 'Yes, it's the good life, mate.'

Beautiful. And so indeed it must be, if you have known what it's like to be a refugee from Lebanon, or the poverty of a village in the countryside of Croatia.

8
Sydney

'The nation was built on the principle that for every family there should be a separate house and for every person there should be a separate room . . . Australia is the small house. Ownership of one in a fenced allotment is as inevitable and unquestionable a goal of the average Australian as marriage . . . This is the story of a material triumph and an aesthetic calamity.'
(Robin Boyd, Australian architectural historian)

Eileen is one of 700,000 passengers who commute daily on New South Wales trains and spend that average hour in getting to and from work. Its State Rail Authority claims it carries twice the number of people that travel on all the other state rail systems combined: 220 million a year. Of this number an estimated ninety-eight per cent are Sydney commuters.

Just after half past eight every weekday morning Eileen's waiting on the Parramatta platform for the double-decker tube to glide in. She's thirty-four, recently promoted to be assistant manager of a building society. While the train passes through Lidcombe, Strathfield and those stations with names taken from London suburbia – Stanmore, Lewisham, Croydon – she gets her thoughts in order and reflects in the carriage window on the day ahead. Her great-grandfather was born in Lewisham – the one in England – before emigrating to Sydney. He might have travelled on this Parramatta–Sydney line himself, as it was the first to be made in New South Wales.

Eileen lives ten minutes' drive from Parramatta station, down a cul-de-sac called Jacaranda Drive (part of an estate developed by a contractor in the late sixties), with her husband Peter, a schoolmaster, and her two daughters, Jackie aged seven, and Megan who's ten. You reach the house through a front garden that's nice and sizeable and planted with several trees. It's as if the words that Governor Phillip wrote nearly two centuries before had been specifically intended for their house: 'Land will be granted with a clause that will ever prevent more than one house being built on the allotment, which will be 60 feet in front and 150 feet in depth.' Give or take a few inches, this rule has been observed ever since in Australian housing – except in the case of central Sydney to which Phillip on that occasion, ironically enough, was referring.

To be at the station on time, Eileen has to be up at six-thirty, to have a shower herself and get her two children ready. 'But Peter dozes on until about seven-fifteen, waiting until the shower is free – or so he says,' Eileen explains. 'When he does go off to the bathroom he turns the radio up as loud as possible to listen to one of the dozen or so breakfast radio stations. Garry O'Callaghan on 2UE is very popular, but Peter doesn't like him because he's always interrupting a record to say there's an ambulance heading down the Parramatta road or some police message like that. He prefers Clive Robertson on 2BL. Peter calls himself "an evening person" so Clive is good at sharpening his wits for him in the morning, like when he goes off into his little flights of fantasy for five or ten minutes at a time, and you have to listen carefully to catch all his innuendos.

'We listen to the ABC news together at seven-forty-five usually, or else the commercial news at eight, while we're having breakfast and getting ready. Everyone has coffee and cereal, or grapefruit if Peter is trying to lose weight. Megan has three bowls of her favourite cereal but she doesn't eat much for the rest of the day. As a working mum, you see, I can't spend time cooking hot breakfasts for everyone, but we do make an exception with ham and eggs on Christmas Day. Meanwhile Peter is very good about lending the kids a hand with the sandwiches they're going to take to school: Jackie likes baked beans best, or processed cheese or beetroot sandwiches. Then we're off about eight-twenty, me in my Toyoto Corolla (second-hand of course) and Peter in his Mazda Sedan with the kids in the back.'

Although it may not appear anything so dramatic, this is part of what has been called 'the greatest social change in post-war Australian life'. Before the Second World War, the rule was that the only women who worked were unmarried ones. A wife's place was in the home, cooking hot breakfasts, taking the kids to school, doing the housework, and giving birth to children – the first of which arrived, on average, between one and two years after marriage. But now Eileen goes off to work, and so do forty-three and a half per cent of married women in Australia (as of October 1982). She shares the housework, with her husband and with labour-saving gadgetry; she doesn't waste time cooking breakfast. And on average the modern Australian wife now gives birth to her first child *five* years after marriage, thanks to the fact that she has a job as well as contraception. This seems to be an enormous development to have occurred within the space of one generation of any society, let alone in one which has prided itself on its machismo and was – in terms of demographic fact – male-dominated until after the Second World War.

'Peter's school is almost next door to Jackie and Megan's primary, and with a bit of luck he'll find somewhere to park that's close to the main buildings of his school. But the shortage of parking space is terrible – it's so bad that it's always coming up on the agenda at staff meetings. Cups of coffee and a few chats about the afternoon's sport tend to keep Peter going through the lessons of the morning. Then he joins in the school lunch or has his sandwiches, because a pub counter-lunch wouldn't be quite the thing and a business lunch in a restaurant would be too expensive.

'Jackie and Megan get back to the car park about half past three but often they have to wait around a while until Peter's ready to run them home. If it's Friday afternoon they'll go to the No Frills supermarket in Parramatta to do the weekly shop – Peter says it's more convenient for him to pop in there for a couple of hours after school than for me to go out again after I've got home from work. We budget about a hundred dollars a week on food for the four of us – about ten dollars on vegetables, seven dollars on milk, twenty on meat, the rest on tins. Peter says the No Frills range is comprehensive and good value; he reckons it works out at about fifteen per cent cheaper than in ordinary shops.

'If it's hot, the kids go off to a neighbour's to use their swimming pool when they get home – several of our neighbours have a pool, but no one has a private tennis court yet, that's the next stage upwards. Peter might do the lawn with the flymo while waiting for me to return, and if he's unlucky the wife next door yoo-hoos at him over the fence and forces him to have a chat. He can't very well tell her to push off as she sends her son to his school, and it's worse if it's sunny because she'll be out in her bikini to let everyone see that she had her breasts done recently – not an uplifting experience for Peter though. Her husband's a dentist, by the way. On the other side of the fence there's a couple who are state school teachers, then – as you go round the Drive – a chemist, an electrician, an engineer, a doctor, and a taxi driver who was a professional too until he managed to raise the taxi licence fee of fifty-five thousand dollars and bought his own business. They're all married couples, of course; you can't manage the mortgage repayments on these sort of houses if you're a single person.

'How friendly are we with them? Well, it's quite difficult getting the balance right. I mean at Christmas, for example, Peter invites most of our neighbours around for a drink – and you have to specify that it's for a drink so that they're friendly but not too friendly, if you see what I mean. The engineer and his wife are our only actual friends who come round for dinner. Of course we always say hello to any neighbours we bump into but we might not see some of them from one community carol-singing to the next. There's no local association of residents or anything, but we rally round in a crisis – if someone dies, say, then everyone is friendly enough to lend a hand. And Peter thinks it stupid that some neighbours are too proud to ask and borrow something: he's always ready to ask for the loan of a spanner or spade!

'When I get home in the evenings – and supposing the

train's on time – we have tea at six o'clock. With a bit of luck the milk should have arrived by then, though you can't be sure with these afternoon deliveries they're introducing, now that they've got these new containers which can stand in the sun for hours without affecting the milk, supposedly. Most milkmen tend to be migrants, doing it as a second job, although it costs twenty to thirty thousand dollars to buy a milk run. A fishman also comes to the Drive once a week. The post, if we've got any, comes late morning or early afternoon.'

For tea Eileen says she normally cooks a grill – maybe sausages or steak, with a salad in summer or vegies in winter, followed by ice cream with topping for the kids. About once a week they might bring home some pizzas or go out to their nearest McDonalds. Peter and Eileen find that casseroles are convenient in winter 'because we can get a couple of meals out of them'. Afterwards it is bath-time. Megan is old enough to have her bath by herself (soon she'll be graduating to showers in the morning), but Mum keeps an eye on Jackie. Then they watch some television till eight-thirty, or play with the new electronic game Megan was given for her last birthday present. Then it's bed for them, a beer for Peter, and a few small jobs for Eileen.

If they've arranged a dinner for the weekend Eileen takes the cookbook out and makes an effort to try something special. Having soup makes it seem like an imposing lot of cutlery on the table, and she'll do a roast of beef or lamb, or a chicken done in sauce – and a bottle of wine (never a cask) with an interesting label. Peter likes a chocolatey pudding, then coffee with brown sugar. Port follows in many households but Peter swears by muscat.

When they are alone in bed again Peter and Eileen may have to talk about the holidays – this year they might only be able to afford to go camping, if Peter's friend can lend them a tent, that is – or about their parents, and decide that it's time to have them all round next Sunday for afternoon tea. Money's a worry too, because although both of them work – Eileen bringing in eighteen thousand dollars a year from her building society job and Peter twenty-five thousand dollars – they are not what you would call affluent. They have a dish-washer, because it's a blessing for Eileen, but they don't have a deep freeze yet, only a separate compartment in the refrigerator. And not only do they have a car each to run (Peter's will cost him one hundred and seventy dollars a month for four years to repay), they've also got the mortgage of three hundred and sixty dollars a month, house insurance of two hundred and twenty dollars a year, the life assurance which varies between five hundred and a thousand dollars a year, and their five-hundred-and-sixty-dollar annual Medibank contribution to cover for the health of the four of them. It all adds up; plus, there's the old Bankcard, that fatal bit of plastic so easy to wave when you want something. Nearly four million Australians have one, and the average amount they owed at the end of 1982 was four hundred and sixty dollars each – incurring interest at the rate of ten per cent per month. A good deal of Australian affluence therefore is credit-based.

'So we've stopped taking a newspaper every day, and just get the *Herald* delivered on Saturdays – the newsagent comes round in his car and tosses it, all wrapped up, out of his window into our garden. It may not have much news in it but there are the car and property sections: Peter likes looking out for something to swap for his Mazda Sedan, though he usually has to make do with buying some new accessory instead, like a roof rack. It's not all eating out and parties in Jacaranda Drive, you know.'

Who would play God and pass judgement on the Australian suburb? One trouble is the dearth of scientific evidence on which to base an opinion more profound or less sweeping than 'definitely a Good Thing' or 'cultural deserts the lot of them'. Sociology is fairly recent in Australia: up until the mid-1960s only three out of twelve universities had sociology departments, and two of those were bracketed with anthropology. As one of the authors of *Australian Society* remarks: 'Perhaps there is some cultural significance in this scholarly neglect of, and apparent blindness to, the most physically obvious and socially dominant mode of Australian society.'

The architect Hugh Stretton has offered perhaps the most strenuous defence of the suburb. While acknowledging that 'the culture of assembly and conspiracy, of theatre and gallery and café, of great newspapers and little magazines, of chance encounters and intellectual colonies, is rarely strong in a commuters' city', he argues that suburbs have unrivalled advantages of lifestyle. If they are all so similar, each house fractionally different but basically the same, that according to him is because 'more and more people are at last getting what all of them have always, freely, independently, identically wanted'. And, he goes on to add, there is scope for creative individuality in suburbia. It can be found, for instance, in cooking or in arranging the suburban quarter-acre of garden. Hmm.

In summary, Stretton gives the suburb generous references:

> It reconciles access to work and city with private, adjustable, self-expressive living space at home. Plenty of adults love that living space, and sub-divide it ingeniously. For children it really has no rivals. At home it can allow them space, freedom and community with their elders; they can still reach bush and beach in one direction and in the other, schools to educate them and cities to sophisticate them. About half the lives of most of us are spent growing up then bringing others up. Suburbs are good places to do it, precisely because they let the generations co-exist, with some continuing independence for each. These are the gains our transport costs buy for us.

One flaw at least can be detected in this argument, about the generations co-existing. Researchers have found that the residents of a suburb tend to move in at roughly the same stage after marriage, and to grow old together. The children of that suburb then form what is known as a 'ripple effect' by leaving, when grown up, for a newer suburb further out where housing is cheaper and therefore nearer their price-range (and the journey to work even longer). So older, car-less couples may be left behind in their inner circle, without any communal places in which to meet people, as they would have in the city. Grandfather, father, son, as you move out from the centre.

In this regard a Gallup International Survey of 1977 is significant, because it asked people in various continents what their chief fear or worry for the future was. One per cent of Africans said that loneliness was their chief fear (money, food, etc., being more pressing concerns); three per cent of Americans and Far Easterners said loneliness; and six per cent of Australians. The only country to match this fear of loneliness, with six per cent as well, was the United Kingdom which, in the beginning, inspired Australia with the desire for privacy in a house with a fence around it.

Homogeneity, a basic sameness, is another criticism of the suburb. But Lyn Richards — the sociologist who thinks that women working is the biggest change in post-war Australian society — has, since the late seventies, been studying the life of a Melbourne suburb (the one she considered the most average she could find); and has discovered, to her surprise, that it is not homogeneous at all. Indeed, differences are all too quickly established as residents move into their new suburb. Petty distinctions are created between native Australians and immigrants, between those with built-in swimming pools and those with above-ground pools and those without either. Or a house 'up the hill' — which turns out to be a barely perceptible rise in the ground, with views at the top scarcely worth a second look — is valued at twenty thousand dollars more than an identical one (except in social standing) at the bottom of the same road. There *is* variety of weave in a suburban tapestry, she says. But you have to look more closely than elsewhere in order to appreciate it.

Alexander Buzo, Sydney playwright, admits: 'I used to be one of those who said about suburbia, "Oh, cultural deserts," when I was in my twenties. But now I guess it is better to live in Hibiscus Avenue and wash the car every Sunday morning than to smoke pot in communes or join a far-out religious group. The alternatives that have been tried in Australia don't seem to have been any improvement on suburbia.'

143

Max Harris, literary and social critic, likes Australia's placid society: 'I would not have our Australia other than it is, for peace sake, amen . . . but we have to acknowledge that the price paid is cultural insipidity.' And if Australians are the most suburbanised of peoples – the statistic is that almost seventy per cent live in suburbanised cities (not even counting towns), more than in any comparable country – it might be reasonably deduced that suburbia has played a part in creating this peace-at-the-expense-of-insipidness. 'We are sleep-walking. That may be a condition of the peaceable kingdom. I don't mind sleep-walkers. But I wouldn't want my daughter to marry one.'

Maybe, however, the whole argument about suburbia has been made redundant by recession. Fewer and fewer young couples can afford a large mortgage at high interest rates, so they make do with a flat or apartment nearer the city centre. The dream of owning your own home may or may not have been questioned, but that is irrelevant if there is not enough money to pay for one. The brilliant Boyd hit the nail again with his prophecy in 1968: 'Inevitably the Australian ideal of a five-roomed detached villa for every family will recede further during the remaining years of the century. It will be threatened by more flats, perhaps a revival of terraces . . . by cluster housing and other multiple dwelling types yet to be invented. One day historians may decide that the heyday of the private separate house was the first half of the twentieth century.' If that is so, the suburb will decline with it.

But for the moment the suburbs continue to thrive, the parents to commute and the children to grow up in fresh air and clean surroundings. Jackie and Megan are said to be perfectly happy with their home: 'They love it here. They'd hate to move to a city apartment.' So their parents keep earning the wherewithal and, in Eileen's case, travelling many miles to do so. Ten hours a week she spends in train and car, time that might as well go down as wasted. And why does she make this sacrifice? For her children. It's a form of heroism, certainly of altruism. In a way not to be sneezed at, I suppose the old Australian virtues have been adapted to modern living.

9
Sydney to Moree

'Their cultural background does not allow them to compete in a society where the main objective is material acquisition.'
(Phillip Segal, white solicitor employed by the Aboriginal Legal Service in Moree, N.S.W.)

In the end carriage of the North-West Tablelands Express as it neared Moree, a Dostoevsky-ish scene presented itself. Three plump children of a plumper mother had been sitting together since the train had left Sydney early that morning. Mother and eldest daughter sat in adjoining seats, though there was scarcely room; opposite them, two younger daughters, all the shape of barrels. At frequent intervals mother or eldest daughter would lean forward to slap the youngest with a sandal, tipping the seat forward so that both were on the verge of capsizing on the carriage floor. The middle daughter, the nearest to shapely – about twelve in years and stone – surveyed these proceedings and ate. The youngest, whenever assailed, would scream out loud, and the more she screamed the more they slapped her; and having screamed, the more she consumed of crisps, chocolate and cans of fizzy drink for consolation. So it had gone on, scream and ice cream, through the day.

We had come over the lovely Hawksbury River, past Newcastle, and its open-cut mines, up through the Liverpool Ranges and on to the north-west plains of New South Wales, where lakes aplenty danced in the distance but contained not a drop to drink. A pleasant grandmother, in the carriage as far as Werris Creek, said she knew friends who had just slaughtered 2,500 Merino sheep when the cost of bore-water and hand-feeding rose too high. What should have been lush, beyond the Great Dividing Range, was sere.

This grandmother thought that the overnight North-West Mail, and its daytime equivalent the North-West Tablelands Express, had not changed in her fifty years of travelling on it; she said as much when her coffee lurched and went flying over her skirt. Australian rolling-stock seems to be either very modern or very old: this was not the very modern kind. At lunchtime a waitress came round with a menu and fixed an antique board to each seat as a table. The family of four tucked in; and when they had finished, temporarily, their mother remarked to the pleasant grandmother that there had been a trial lately in Moree, after a young Aborigine named McIntosh had been shot during a brawl that had got seriously out of hand. Donald Horne had said there had been no race-riot in modern Australia, not since the 1930s when there were 'dago hunts' in Kalgoorlie (without any fatalities). But what happened in Moree had been widely labelled a race-riot.

As the afternoon heated up, the train stopped at wayside halts and outback towns with names that could only have been Australian: Breeza, Baanbaa, Narrabri, Edgeroi. A wooden hut served for each station, a two-storey verandahed pub for each settlement. It was nine hours' travelling before the Express terminated in Moree, strictly East Moree. Clouds were building up, and lightning flashed at the far edge of the plain, inaudible, without rain falling, while blowaway grass scudded down the empty street outside the station. Each plant is the size of a starfish, blades of grass radiating from its centre; several of these blowaway grasses stopped in the gutters of Moree and paused, before the scudding wind blew them on.

Moree's prosperity was founded on sheep, and on wheat grown in the rich black soil of the north-west plains. Families, descendants of the original squatters, owned the land and employed plenty of casual labour around their farms. There was all the work involved in harvesting to be done, and grain to be delivered to the railhead. In other seasons of the year fences had to be mended, sheep sheared and crutched; or there was 'stick-picking', a euphemism for clearing the logs off newly claimed land. Mixed-blood Aborigines drifted towards Moree from a wide catchment area to obtain this work. They competed for it with the local poor whites, but normally there was enough to go round.

This pattern began to change during the 1950s. From small-time family ownership the farms moved under the control of national and multinational companies. Their programme was a large swift input of capital, mechanisation, and a large swift profit. Thus they did away with sheep altogether; they introduced bulk-handling of wheat which took the grain directly from field to silo; they planted – outside the wheat season – sorghum, milo, sun flower and millet, which do not need much attention, to speed up a return on their investment. All these processes were introduced at the expense of jobs. Eventually the ultimate stage was reached, whereby one man in a tractor was guided by a laser beam and a computer.

The one new crop which did create more jobs was cotton, once American and Japanese financiers had been attracted to the idea by the soil and by the possibilities of irrigation from subsidised bore holes. Cotton chippers were now wanted to go along the rows of cotton, each up to two miles long, and 'chip' away the weeds. Casual labourers – Aboriginal women amongst them – could thus earn thirty-five to thirty-eight dollars for a long day in the summer sun, but cotton-chipping only provided employment for two or at most three months of the year. Otherwise, there was little other work available by November 1982. With the running-down of the sheep industry, an abattoir on the outskirts of Moree had been closed in 1980, at the cost of 300 jobs; the persisting drought put more and more farm workers on the dole. Unofficial estimates were that ninety per cent of Aboriginal men in town were by then without regular employment, and half the total of poor whites.

Best of all jobs, for those Aborigines who had drifted to Moree before 1968, were those on the state railways. The railways were exceptional in that they paid equal wages before Aborigines were made Australian citizens and the payment of equal wages thus became legally enforceable. Aboriginal railway employees were also allowed to join a union; otherwise, only Aboriginal shearers could do so. On the railways they were mostly employed as fettlers, a few as guards, and such work gave them an idea of what it was like to have a permanent job – and what it was like not to be dependent upon the whims of a white farm boss. Some settled in so completely that they were recognised as all but equals by their fellow Australians: 'he's got a white heart' was the final seal of approval. But some of these Aborigines who made it in white society were regarded as Uncle Toms: 'coconut blacks' was the derogatory phrase used by Aborigines themselves in the north-west, to describe those who were black outside and white inside.

For those Aborigines – or 'Murris' as they call themselves – who conformed with white values, the reward was a citizen's pass. This was bestowed on Aboriginal servicemen who had acquitted themselves well in the Second World War, and on other upstanding examples of their race of the 'Jackey-Jackey' type who had been recognised as 'faithful'. With a citizen's pass – or a dog licence as it was known in the vernacular – an Aborigine could enter a hotel and be served alcohol. Otherwise an Aborigine found in possession of alcohol was liable to a fine of ten pounds (no small sum before 1968), and a citizen's pass-holder who supplied alcohol could be fined up to fifty pounds and lose his licence.

While this carrot was offered to those who thought of conforming to white values, there were means of taking the stick to those who did not. A child could be taken into the care of the (now-extinct) Aboriginal Protection Board without any reason being given to his or her parents. Such children would be sent first to a home or training camp, far from their family or any concentration of Aborigines, there to become Christians and trained as domestic servants or jackeroos. Local farmers could then apply to these homes, and by promising to provide a decent Christian environment, obtain from them a cheap supply of labour in return for 'pocket money' which might not always be paid.

If they went to the cinema in Moree, Aborigines sat together at the front and were segregated from the white clientele. But in this respect Moree's open-air cinema was an improvement on the one in another country town where they were separated by an electric fence. Certain shop-keepers refused to serve Aboriginal customers; others might make them wait if there was a white customer behind them in the queue. Taxis belonging to the RSL Club in Moree refused to carry Aboriginal passengers, even though there was no public transport available.

Nor was Moree's local council renowned as progressive in the question of race relations. After the war it came to be dominated by the merchants who moved into Moree to supply the expanding agricultural industry and the multi-national companies which were taking over. They belonged to the Masons or the Rotary or the Apex Clubs, and the local chamber of commerce. The values which they promoted in the council chamber were reinforced by these institutions.

A growing number of Australian country towns are relieved by an open-air Olympic-size pool, a welcoming sight to dusty travellers from afar. Moree was amongst the first to construct one, along with two spa baths filled with hot water that came gushing from the ground. In 1955 the Moree council passed a resolution that Aborigines should not be allowed to enter this complex of pool and baths.

There were always, however, in Moree as in the rest of Australia, some whites attempting to assist rather than hamper the native inhabitants, their efforts culminating locally in the creation of an Aboriginal Advancement Committee about the same time that the council was passing its swimming-pool legislation. A kindergarten was started by the Committee; the Catholic Church established a mission to offer medical and educational services as well as Christianity; the Aboriginal Protection Board erected some thirty houses, followed by the Housing Commission offering more. But the vast majority of Aborigines continued to live along the banks of the Mehi River in over-crowded humpies, and roughly divided themselves into three camps: Stanley Village, Mehi Mission, and Bottom Camp. Until the late sixties the only place where Moree's whites and Aborigines lived side by side was in Maud Street or 'Soapy Row', outside the local soap factory.

Then one day in February 1965 the Freedom Rides began. Inspired by events in the United States, bus-loads of 'Freedom Riders' from Sydney University came to town and protested against the Moree Council's discrimination. (Ever since, 'trendy southern lefties' have not been amongst the town's most welcome visitors.) This publicity was effective: three months later the council was embarrassed into lifting its ban on blacks using the spa baths, since when children of all shades have splashed together in the waters. During the next decade (the seventies) the hostile stares – when an Aborigine entered a white domain – started to disappear and racial discrimination became less overt.

Gradually, too, the Aboriginal population increased until Moree had 3,000 of them, as large a community as any Australian town. Only a handful were full-bloods; the rest were products of some white liaison, hastily begotten, hastily forgotten. They had left – or been driven out of – their tribal homeland and had drifted towards Moree, arriving with their native culture as diluted as their blood. Nowadays they leave school without prospects, hang round the pubs or milk bars, and spend their twenty-cent pieces on electronic video games that ping, whizz and zoom hour after hour, in place of the corroboree music their ancestors knew. And this younger generation became far more politically active than their fathers had ever been. Perhaps the loudest expression of it came during the committal hearing after McIntosh's death, when a young activist said in court that authority in Aboriginal affairs had always been in white hands and 'not after 200 years of colonisation do I appreciate [white] authority'. The public gallery, crowded with Aborigines, exploded into applause.

A two-year cycle developed: in 1976, 1978 and 1980 there were pub-brawls on such a violent scale as to attract outside media attention to the town. One side would happen to be composed of whites and the other of Aborigines, but they weren't labelled as race-riots. These outbursts seemed to be caused by the heat as much as anything, since they always occurred in summer, when paint would bubble up from the walls and the thermometer would regularly hit the mid-forties centigrade. Moree is another of those places in Australia where birds are said to fall from the sky.

By November 1982 the weather was hot again. It was also the height of the cotton-chipping season, which meant there was a little more money about for spending on Christmas presents – and on drink. Hot winds blew down the main street; the blowaway grass bowled along, before hesitating in the dust. Everyone waited for the tension to be relieved by the next blood-letting, in the absence of any rain to dampen down the earth.

Imperial Buildings, dated 1929, extend down the main street of Moree in a style reminiscent of the upper deck of a steamer, before making a right-angle turn along Heber Street. Two-storeyed the whole way along, the buildings upstairs have a white-washed frontage with a continuous verandah fenced in by some cheap railing; downstairs the frontage has been up-dated to suit the image of a couple of boutiques, chemists and a milk bar. The Imperial Hotel itself has two modernised entrances facing on to Heber Street. One leads to the Captain Cook Bar, which has a carpet and some pretensions to refined behaviour; the other entrance is to the Ned Kelly Bar. They say it's the custom for whites to drink mostly in the Captain Cook and Aborigines in the Ned Kelly – since 1968, that is, when Aborigines were permitted to drink alcohol – but that was never a clear-cut distinction. The same overlapping would occur in marriage: a few poor whites in Moree had Aboriginal wives, and an increasing number of white women took 'Murri' husbands.

A certain lawlessness, appropriately enough, character-ised the Ned Kelly. During the drought marihuana became one of the area's few cash crops, and even more blind eyes than usual were turned in a period of recession. It is said that anyone going to a number of hotels in Moree has only to inquire about 'cigarette papers' for transactions in marihuana to be conducted in that hotel's lavatory. Probably more whites than Aborigines sell it, and more Aborigines than whites smoke it. By 1982 the trade was going on so openly that some well-known drug dealers, labelling themselves 'unemployed', were confident enough to take to court dissatisfied clients who had done them violence. Certain hotel-keepers and their sons were reportedly doing more than turn a blind eye.

But there had been no trouble in the Imperial when its publican was a thin, short, cool-witted landlady who knew exactly the moment to put her foot down. On her retirement though, she expressed the opinion that her successor would be too abrasive to be diplomatic if tempers flared; she always said, privately, that there was going to be trouble.

'Cheeky' McIntosh was of the Boggabilla people. Boggabilla is the next town north of Moree, much smaller, where the passenger trains used to terminate before the railhead was cut back to Moree. The McIntosh family had followed the railhead south on the grounds that there was more Aboriginal housing in Moree, and a slightly better chance of a job.

His grandfather is said to have looked Scottish, but to have spoken the Boggabilla language and to have been tribal-minded; his grandmother was dark, and together they produced a range of children who covered the spectrum of shades, which is not unusual. Cheeky's mother became religious – officially Anglican although preferring a Pentecostal approach. (Of all the Christian denominations that claim Aboriginal followers, only the Roman Catholics and Pentecostalists have a significant number of practising Aborigines. The Catholics actually have one Aboriginal priest, who tends to the charismatic; the Pentecostals find their fervent approach comes closer than that of any other Christian group to native spiritualism.)

Cheeky got his nickname from being a bit of a wild boy in his early teens. He had a court record – but that is not very remarkable considering that in the year prior to his death there had been 1,223 Aboriginal juvenile offences, and 1,269 Aboriginal adult offences, tried in the Moree

'The road forms a very amusing transit to a stranger, for as you rise the incline the prisoners puff and blow pushing on the carriage but when descending up they jump alongside of you and away you go, dashing, crashing, tearing on.' (Captain Stonor, *A Year in Tasmania*)

Trappers in 'Tiger Country', the West Coast of Tasmania.

Norman Cowans, England's Jamaican-born fast-bowler, triumphant after England's three-run victory over Australia at Melbourne, January 1983.

Largest cricket ground in the world, the M.C.G. was also used for the Olympic Games of 1956. The first of all Test matches was played here in 1877, when it was known as Richmond Paddock; and the highest of all first-class totals, Victoria's 1107 against New South Wales, was made here in 1926/7.

One of the remaining
forty thousand full-
blood Aborigines.

A hand-out of
supplies for New
South Wales
Aborigines in the
1880s. The era of
dependence had
already started.

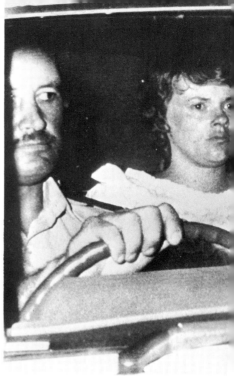

Two faces of Lindy Chamberlain, the focus of attention in Australia's most famous – and lengthy – *cause célèbre*.

End of the trail.

court of petty sessions – out of a town population of 3,000 Aborigines. Most of the offences were petty, and not a few could be attributed to the attitude of the police, which might reasonably be called unenlightened rather than malicious (however, the Aborigines were impressed by the difference in integrity when the Homicide Squad flew in from Sydney). In any event, Cheeky was said to be growing up, to be putting some of his wild ways behind him.

According to his friend Cecil Craigie, who gave evidence at the committal proceedings, he and Cheeky had gone first to the Victoria Hotel on the evening of November 4. The Victoria is the railwaymen's pub just across the road from the station in East Moree. A few Aborigines always used to mix in there because it's close to Stanley Village, and it was no different this night. When it came to closing time, Craigie and friends went over the main bridge into Moree itself, to the Imperial Hotel about a mile away, to have another drink there and play pool.

Soon after their arrival a brawl ensued, according to the new publican of the Imperial, Ian Bowen. Giving evidence later at the murder committal hearing, Bowen recalled: 'I told him [Craigie] to leave the bar. He then swore at me and I went down to the other end of the bar and picked up a pool cue.' Both Craigie and McIntosh had been barred from the Ned Kelly Bar for violent behaviour in the past. Bowen testified that there were now about one hundred patrons inside (though other estimates were lower), including Steven Gregory Delamothe, aged twenty-one, and Warren John Ledingham, twenty-seven.

At ten-thirty that evening Bowen rang the police. Senior Constable Laurie Smith answered the call at the police station where he was alone, the other two constables on duty having been called out of town. Smith therefore had to go by himself to the Imperial. On entering the Ned Kelly he saw a group of Aborigines and told them: 'Come on you blokes, you know you're barred, you will have to leave.' Smith, apparently not thinking himself equal to this situation on his own, then left and returned not long afterwards with his Inspector. But by then some damage had been done. When Smith returned he found 'the bar had been extensively damaged, pool tables had been thrown upside down, windows broken and on the floor there was a large amount of broken glasses, broken billiard cues and pool balls were scattered everywhere'. Bowen alleged that in addition a garbage tin had been thrown through his front windows and empty beer kegs rammed through the windows of a bottle shop at the rear of his hotel.

There are conflicting views about how the violence escalated, about the numbers of each side, and whether one or two Aborigines started to chant, 'Land rights, land rights!' inside the bar. But it would seem agreed that some Aborigines in town, hearing of the brawl, forced their way into the Ned Kelly Bar to help their friends, and that the fight subsequently spilled out into Roslyn Lane which runs beside the Imperial to Heber Street, and parallel to the main street. So far these events were no different from previous pub-brawls in Moree, and of a similar pattern to many more which have happened in country towns, sparked by a publican – often no doubt justifiably – refusing to serve one or two Aborigines, but then extending that ban to cover all of them in his bar.

Such happenings thus far on the evening of November 4 were all too typical; those on the early hours of November 5 were unique in recent Australian history. When the fighting spilled into Roslyn Lane towards midnight, white men and youths chased the Aborigines down it. At the bottom of Roslyn Lane they turned right, and then first left into Endeavour Lane which leads down to the Mehi River. Fleeing down Endeavour Lane the Aborigines passed Taylor Oval, a cricket ground, on their left. On their right was a primary school. Both these extended about half down the 300-yard lane, until the Oval gave way to some tennis courts surrounded by wire netting. At the bottom of the lane the ground fell away at what is called a levy bank, into a field which is flooded periodically by the river (or strictly creek) but at that season was of course dry. Having run halfway down Endeavour Lane, the Aborigines halted and decided to make their stand.

They could in fact hardly choose anywhere else, since their three possible escape routes were quickly blocked.

Along the river bank in one direction was a little-used crossing occupied by whites. In the other direction, the bridge carrying the main street over to East Moree was guarded too. Most of the Aborigines lived in East Moree and therefore wanted to cross it to go home. Meanwhile a third group of whites stood at the end of Endeavour Lane. So the Aborigines could but wait beside the primary school and the tennis courts until their enemies had dispersed.

As for weapons, both sides had seized whatever impromptu arms that had lain to hand. Next day broken planks, iron bars, a golf club and a broken billiard cue were found in Endeavour Lane, while alongside the tennis courts wooden seats, a tennis umpire's stool and garbage tins were found, all of which appeared to have been burnt. Around one-thirty a.m., however, the balance of power was dramatically altered.

A few days later, after being arrested in Inverell, a third white youth, Geoffrey Leigh Willmott, told the police: 'It all started at the pub – there was a big blue and Steven Delamothe got a belting. Him and a bloke called Warren then asked me to drive them home. I drove them back and parked near the bowling club and they left me and I heard some shots fired.' The bowling club stands beside the main street near the bridge. From there it is a short walk along the river bank to the tennis courts at the bottom of Endeavour Lane.

The guns which Willmott had driven the pair home to collect were a 30–30 Winchester and a .22 rifle. Ledingham later admitted to being the owner of both, after they had been recovered from the Mehi River. (Licences for rifles, but not hand-guns, are easily obtainable in country towns.)

While these three were absent from the Imperial Hotel collecting Ledingham's two rifles, McIntosh had also disappeared from the scene of the fight. He had somehow crossed the river to Moree Hospital, standing in open ground on the other side, and was there treated before midnight for lacerations to his right eyebrow, thumb and left ankle. Afterwards he returned to the fray and joined his fellow Aborigines in Endeavour Lane, talking and waiting, until Willmott's car drew up at the bowling club. From there Delamothe and Ledingham went quietly to the levy bank at the bottom end of the lane.

Delamothe later led police to the scene of the shooting, where he said: 'I was lying here and Warren was here. We lay there for about five minutes and then we fired over their heads.' They fired round after round over the top of the levy bank, which served as cover for them exactly like a trench, and through the tennis courts to where the Aborigines were scattered by the school wall. The distance was about one hundred yards. A Winchester has a range of 3,000 feet; a .22 of about 1,800 feet.

Ledingham, after giving himself up three days later, told police: 'I only fired one shot lying down. I had to kneel up to fire the gun. We did not mean to kill anyone, we just meant to scare them.' Whatever their intentions, their bullets poured into the school wall as the Aborigines tried to scramble over it and the tennis-court fence to safety.

A seventeen-year-old, Warren Tighe, was hit in the shoulder. McIntosh died instantly. A bullet from the Winchester rifle entered his right shoulder, punctured a lung and went through his heart, before coming to rest in muscle tissue. When Ledingham and Delamothe ceased firing and the white blockaders had dispersed, his body was taken to the hospital covered in blood. There were no signs of life. He was nineteen.

In the same week that Cheeky McIntosh was killed, a local Aborigine was appointed to the board of the Moree Hospital for the first time. Human progress can be like that: one step forward, one step back.

On November 11, 1982, McIntosh's funeral was held in the Anglican Church of All Saints. It is situated – ironically enough – at the head of Endeavour Lane where the bullet-holes in the school wall are still evident. At the graveside Father Richard Buckhorn, a radical Catholic priest from the parish of Boggabilla, gave the following address:

We who live out on these western plains know how storm-clouds gather; how pressure builds up at some point in that cloud, until lightning flashes down to some point on earth, thunder roars, and life-giving rain is released.

There are many people in Australia who live in harmony, accepting one another as equals. But there is also a cloud of racism which hangs over this country. At times it gathers into a storm-cloud; the pressure of anger and hatred build up. And in the early hours of last Friday morning, thunder roared and lightning flashed across Taylor Oval, and struck down the young man whose body we now lay to rest.

But why did it have to be Cheeky? And why now? Just as tall objects and buildings attract lightning, perhaps it is because more Aboriginal people are choosing to walk tall, to fight for their rights, to demand that they be treated as human beings with dignity and pride. Perhaps it is because of this that racism is showing itself more openly, more viciously.

And this is nothing new! Eighteen years ago, Martin Luther King was cut down by an assassin's bullet in Memphis, Tennessee, USA. Why? Because he dared to have a dream, and strive to make that dream come true.

One hundred and thirty-three years ago, Gibber, an Aboriginal leader of the Kamilaroi Tribe, was shot. This happened in the area from which some of Cheeky's people come: perhaps he was one of his ancestors. He was resisting the white invasion of the areas now known as the McIntyre River.

Unlike Martin Luther King, we haven't any of the words he spoke. We haven't the names of the other Aboriginals who died fighting for that land. It's almost as if white society has considered to deprive Aboriginal people of any memory of their own heroes: and this is a country where the words 'Lest We Forget' are emblazoned on monuments, and the walls of RSL Clubs.

And nearly 2,000 years ago, another man was killed. If Jesus were alive today, he would again be condemned as an agitator, a trouble-maker. He was at the centre of a triumphal street march into Jerusalem on Palm

157

Sunday – and probably without a permit under the Traffic Act.

I believe that this wounded world can be healed by the blood of Jesus: and that because of him, any blood shed in a situation of injustice, in any struggle for justice, can heal us. Our world has been healed by the blood of Martin Luther King. And I believe that it can be healed by the blood that poured out of Cheeky in Endeavour Lane last Friday morning.

As Isaiah said, 'We had all gone astray like sheep, each taking his own way', looking after ourselves, failing to care for one another. Rather than fighting racial oppression, we fight one another.

If Cheeky's blood is not to be shed in vain – if this grain of wheat which has died, and we are about to plant in this grave, is to yield a harvest – it is going to depend on us: on each one of us. There is no one here today, black or white, who does not have a part to play in making his blood a healing blood.

We need our dreams: and adapting what Martin Luther King said to this situation here, I want to say to you that I have a dream. I have a dream that one day, in these western plains, all the children of those who dispossessed them of their land, and all who have come since, will be able to sit down together at the table of brotherhood.

I wish to God that I could say that this will be the last time an Aboriginal will be shot in Australia.

But one thing I can say for sure is this: if we allow fear of criticism, of abuse, of being hassled, of being bashed – and even of being killed – if we allow those fears to stop us working to make that dream come true, then it will never come true. We do not seek these things: but Jesus said that those who follow him will be persecuted in the cause of right.

But I do believe that if we who are here today, handful that we are, do not falter in our duty, we will be able to end this racial nightmare, and change the history of this town, this country – and even of the world.

Stan and Val: I know that when you brought Cheeky

into this world, as you cared for him and watched him grow, worried for him – that you never thought that you would come to a day as tragic as this.

But it doesn't matter how long a man lives. What matters is what he achieves. And I believe that Cheeky, by being where he was when that storm-cloud burst, has touched more lives, and achieved more for this world than most of us here will achieve in a lifetime.

After the thunder and lightning comes the rain. The flood of tears that has flowed over these days, that will be shed over this seed we are planting here today, are part of that rain. The clap of thunder that echoed round this land last Friday has shaken and shocked many people of goodwill. May the sweat of their efforts, and of ours, to fight racism, be added to those tears, to make sure this seed yields the harvest it should.

We are not burying a body: we're planting a seed. And I assure you that I, and I hope everyone here today, will try to make sure that it yields a rich harvest. Let us bow our heads, and conclude with the prayer of St Francis of Assisi:

Lord, make me an instrument of your peace;
where there is hatred, let me sow love;
where there is injury, pardon;
where there is doubt, faith;
where there is despair, hope;
where there is darkness, light;
where there is sadness, joy.

O Divine Master,
grant that I may not so much seek
to be consoled, as to console;
to be understood, as to understand;
to be loved, as to love.

For it is in giving that we receive;
it is in pardoning that we are pardoned;
and it is in dying that we are born
to eternal life.

Lord, we commit to the earth the body of your servant, Ronald McIntosh.

Steven Delamothe and Warren Ledingham were eventually sentenced to seven years' imprisonment each for manslaughter. The jury accepted the defence's claim that they were not shooting directly at specific targets. Geoffrey Willmott received six years.

10
Brisbane to Cairns

The Earth is our Mother,
The giver of life.
The white people must be mad.
What person in their right mind
Would rape their mother?

(Wandjuk Marika)

Brisbane, brightest and brashest of state capitals: its city
centre consists of shopping malls where department stores
blare out news of their latest bargains by microphone
into the street. 'Beautiful hairdriers at 99 dollars! Bargain
accessories at low, low prices! Hurry, hurry, hurry and
save, save, save!'

Brisbane is bodies too. In a land of many superb phys-
iques the young women of Brisbane display some of the
finest. Trollope, however, who surveyed Australian women
for a year and presumably with a little detachment as he
was in his mid-fifties, concluded that: 'they grow quickly,
and are women two years earlier in life than our girls – and
consequently are old women some five years sooner.' In
the century since Trollope sun-worship has increased these
differentials, and the effects of many hours on the beach
can't be wholly concealed by make-up.

One blonde Brisbane friend, of all-too-limited acquaintance, was a magnificently formed twenty-five-year-old –
with a complexion which a European woman would have
hoped to avoid until forty. She spoke of it objectively and
fatalistically, as though her face was no longer part of her.
She had at least enjoyed, she said, her teenage hours in the
sun; now she would concentrate on her career, assured in

the knowledge that men would no longer be after her solely for her looks.

Another drawback to the wonderful climate is that Queensland's rate of skin cancer is claimed to be the highest in the world – which is not surprising when you consider another claim, that the one million Queenslanders living north of Rockhampton form the largest white community in the tropics. It proves fatal for no more than two per cent of its victims but radiation, surgery and liquid nitrogen leave scars on the faces in the street. Nevertheless few people take much notice, even to the extent of wearing hats, not even the blondest of Queensland's many German settlers. They might be more mindful had their Tropic been called Cancer not Capricorn.

Brisbane is warm, honest and efficient. Yellow too. Its beer cans are yellow, the tunics of its department-store girls are yellow, the uniforms of attendants on the Sunlander up to Cairns are yellow. It can also be sub-tropically green after the rains have rinsed the innumerable hills, while many of its roofs are a rusty red and its jacarandas gorgeous. But that's old Brisbane. It has newer suburbs of wires and Kentucky Frieds where the sun shines harshly on yellow bunting. This yellowness may be Brisbane's tribute to the pineapple country that surrounds it – or it could be one of the signs that Queensland under the government of Johannes Bjelke-Petersen has had the makings of a banana republic.

Since it was a police commissioner, Ray Whitrod, who said upon his resignation that Queensland was in danger of becoming a police state, this charge of being authoritarian is not simply an emotive slogan hurled by those whom Bjelke-Petersen chooses to brand as student leftists or Aboriginal militants. Some events in the era of his long government read like Tom Sharpe stories: tales of totalitarianism gone so mad that you would laugh if they weren't true. The destruction of a popular Brisbane hotel in the middle of the night, the police raid on Cedar Bay and the banning of *Playboy* were only a few of several occasions when southern states have wondered whether the 'Deep North' is part of the Phillipines or Pakistan.

Hugh Lunn, Brisbane correspondent of *The Australian* and no axe-grinder, explained the background to Queensland's government in 1979 by analysing its ruling clique of ten National Party Cabinet Ministers: 'The Bjelke-Petersen ten were all men: nine were farmers or graziers and the other was on a cane growers' executive before entering politics. They all left school years before they could be challenged by the complexities of tertiary study. All came from small Queensland towns or rural areas – what most Australians would call the bush. These ten men had by far the highest average age of any state government in Australia – over sixty years . . . No wonder that the official Queensland view of the world has so often been archaic, expressing conservative and simplistic views of complex issues.'

He goes on about this gang of ten: 'Their interests (listed in the official Queensland parliamentary handbook) covered scouts, flying, fishing, horse-racing (three times), football (four), bowls (four), cricket (two), golf, trots, Rotary and one even listed "sugar". About the closest any got to something approaching higher culture was the tourism minister Max Hodges, who listed gardening.' The only member of this enlightened body who had gone through formal study was the education minister, suitably enough – and he had qualified as a mechanical fitter. Membership of the Low Churches was another group characteristic.

Anyone who hasn't been to Australia must wonder what on earth the majority of Queenslanders are like if they keep voting for such an oligarchy of real diehards. The catch of course is that a majority of Queenslanders have never voted for Bjelke-Petersen. Throughout the seventies and into the eighties he and his National Party clung on to government without once receiving as much as thirty per cent of the vote – until the 1983 state election when they recorded thirty-nine per cent – by means of creating rural constituencies inhabited by small numbers of graziers of his own kind. Yet it has to be admitted in his defence that he was only following time-honoured Queensland practice, as the state's Labor government busily gerrymandered just after the Second World War. Democracy can be a little ropey around the Equator, and in the 'Deep North' of Australia it has long been a trifle frayed.

Classic examples of un-democracy are the effective ban on street marches and demonstrations (unless they are pro-Salvation Army or Bjelke-Petersen) and the refusal to apply Daylight Saving Time in line with other eastern states. Thereby he pleased no one (Brisbane having sunsets in high summer as early as six o'clock) except the graziers out west, who happened to be that small minority of voters who kept him in power. The same partiality towards rural interests was evident, much more justifiably, in his subsidies for transport and other costs of outback living. But while the Bjelke-Petersen government has been civilised in its treatment of graziers and farmers, it has been somewhat less so in dealing with some of the rest of Queensland's minorities.

Nevertheless, this government partiality towards the bush has led to the preservation of the extensive system of Queensland Railways. While stations have been closed down in the rest of the country, Queensland has kept about 1,300 going across the state, from Abercorn to Zillmere. The vast majority are wayside halts with a tin shack and no platform, in places where if you miss your train you won't be another till next week, where distances to the next settlement are usually measured in three figures or four, and population density is a matter of square miles to each person not persons to the square mile. But from these stations the grazier can still send his children to school in Charters Towers, his wool to market or his cattle to the abattoir. Queensland has the most lucrative freight business of any government-owned system in Australia; and in the old carriages attached to these freight trains a passenger can still experience the outback as he used to be able to on the Indian-Pacific and the Ghan and the Palmerston to Pine Creek.

But before you take the Sunlander north from Brisbane you have to go south to Surfers Paradise. Surfers is unique. You reach it by driving down the coast on Pacific Highway, past

Industrial Paradise. I'm not sure which of the two Nirvanas is more appealing.

Surfers is the capital of corporal excess, the headquarters of hedonism. Surfers is a second double ice-cream with topping, and letting it all hang out. 'Welcome to the Gold Coast,' say the road signs, 'where life's great – zone of peace.' It's not anti-Australian, however, to consider Surfers Paradise uniquely gross; many good Australians think so too.

While cities go high-rise to fit offices in, Surfers builds high to pack in the holiday-makers. So profuse are the skyscrapers along the beach that, as seen from the sea, the whole horizon resembles a graph of trade figures: exports for January are high, decline until March, climb steeply in April, plummet in June and soar again till December. So many high-rise blocks, and cranes building more, are lining the horizon that it can't be long before there is a continuous stretch of them from Surfers through Broadbeach, Mermaid Beach, Miami Beach, Burleigh Heads, Palm Beach, Currumbin, Coolangatta down to Tweed Heads across the border in New South Wales. Then there'll be a complete graph of export figures for years on end.

I wouldn't mind Surfers Paradise – would simply drive past to the wonderful sugarcane country and mountains of rainforest beyond – were it not for the advertisements on commercial television, in Melbourne particularly, which are designed to lure people to the Gold Coast. The combination of climate and Queensland's abolition of death duties has tempted all too many pensioners to invest in a high-rise apartment as their dream retirement home. Their life savings go on eighty thousand dollars for a bare-minimum unit, or up to a third of a million dollars for a two-bedroom apartment in a tower-block that overlooks the beach; and having been tempted there to start a new life without their family, they have no point of contact with the people on the twenty-three floors below or the fifteen floors above.

'We're creating a monstrosity here,' said one Surfers resident who had been around the world as an Australian naval attaché, 'and we have to keep bringing people in to keep the monster going.' So the advertisers advertise –

glamour girls waving colour brochures at the camera and pointing to the surf below their de luxe apartment – while the lenders lend to help the developers develop. Real-estate language has not shirked its task in tempting the public to buy 'unique units just across the road' (if you can get through the stream of traffic) 'from beautiful beaches' (which by five o'clock, when it's safe enough to go out without getting skin cancer, will be in the shadow of your skyscraper). You don't even have to fool some of the people all the time – once is enough if you wave a pen and contract at them after a beguiling visit to your display home. So long as the skyscraper includes the name Paradise or Pacific or Tropic or Surf or Sunshine or Palm or Beach or Miami, it doesn't matter how soon the paint flakes.

But for the moment everything in Surfers dazzles, from the bunting-strewn arcades to the red fingernails holding an alfresco pizza in the mall. Whole Indian states, let alone villages, could be fed with the food wasted in mass cafeterias. Yet in many of these malls and plazas there is to be found a bakery selling fresh bread made on the premises: so that, strangely enough, where life itself is packaged, the staff of it is fresh and wholesome.

The point about Surfers Paradise and the other resorts of the Gold Coast is not that they are Gulag Archipelagos; they are merely frightful places by comparison with the surrounding countryside and with what they might have been, given a more tasteful exploitation of sea, sun and sand. Then it might conceivably have been a vision of Paradise, while as it is the residents of Surfers have been led to settle for . . . rather less.

The Sunlander from Brisbane to Cairns is the chief of Queensland trains. It's an amiable train too, attracting a more varied clientele than the other long-distance inter-city trains in Australia by reason of being cheaper than the coaches going north, almost as quick until the track becomes a bit rickety towards Cairns, and far more pleasant. It's one of those trains that people wave at.

Its route is not like what one might imagine from the

map, where the line appears to lead straight up the coast. There's not much about it that is straight: the train curves and climbs, often chasing its own tail, detouring around the mangrove swamps and seldom in sight of the sea at all, let alone the Great Barrier Reef ('the biggest living thing'). Ultimately the track's design goes back to the brains behind the Queensland system, an engineer called Mr Fitzgibbon (who sounds like another strong-minded Celt). Queensland was not separated from New South Wales until 1859 but immediately it was it demonstrated its independent spirit by adopting a completely new gauge altogether, the three-foot-six-inch, on Mr Fitzgibbon's recommendation. Correctly, he thought that broad (as in Victoria and South Australia) or standard gauge (in New South Wales) would be too costly for a young and sparsely populated colony to afford, especially if its railways had to cross the Great Dividing Range to the grazing pastures that lay beyond. Thus it was, and Fitzgibbon's narrow gauge worked out at half the price that a broader gauge would have cost. Therefore the Sunlander runs over what is in effect up-dated pioneer track. This becomes alarmingly apparent when you approach a river and see that its bridge is composed of a few trunks of ironwood driven into the riverbed.

No less awesome are the distances involved. The Sunlander normally departs from Brisbane's Roma Street in the early morning and reaches Cairns in the late evening of the following day, without ever leaving the state. And Cairns, while it might be in the FNQ as they say (Far North Queensland), is still nearly a thousand kilometres from the northernmost tip of Cape York. Over lunch on the first day in the restaurant car, when the white cranes outside were meeting up with some cockatoos for a quiet drink by the creeks, I attempted to think of other countries in which it was possible to travel for thirty-six hours without crossing a state or provincial border; and by dinner, when the bush was going through its repertoire of gorgeous colours and the ghost gums were as pale as the flesh of lychees, Russia and the Soviet Union were as far as I'd got. Then Susie sat down.

Susie had left home the day before. She had packed up

everything, arranged for her old Cortina to follow on the next freight train, and was trying to make a go of a new life in the FNQ. She looked mid-thirties. We weren't halfway through a bottle of chilled claret (claret is always chilled on the Sunlander) before the story came out, factually, not searching for sympathy. 'We'd been married for ten years and he started saying some hard things to me. Then one of my best friends moved in with him, into *our* house, and I wasn't going to stand for that, so I just left yesterday without saying goodbye.' She was twenty-nine, though she had the crow's feet of someone nearer forty, and I guessed that some of those hard words must have been on these lines, the facial ones. She had no children; home was, or had been, on the Sunshine Coast north of Brisbane; work was dental nursing when she could find it. As she was going to Ingham, in the centre of sugarcane country, at least she had good career prospects. Anyway, Dirk wasn't thinking of her career prospects.

Good old Dirk was a surf life-saver seated at the next table, and as soon as he overheard that Susie was on the rebound he jumped in after her. He was your archetypal 'surfie': short blond hair parted down the middle and bleached by weekend after weekend on the beach. Dirk said he was meant to keep a look-out for great white sharks – when he wasn't behaving like one himself. But in Queensland, he went on, surf life-savers are mainly there to keep an eye out for 'stingers' (sea-wasps that electrocute) and the occasional sea-snake. Susie was cheered up now, a bit impressed.

Predictably, Dirk thought that Australian life-savers were the best, but several world titles would confirm that he wasn't entirely 'blowing'. He said that in the United States they are professional, but the only time Dirk got paid was in the school holidays when the beaches were crowded: then Dirk's work was rewarded with a hundred dollars a week. For the most part Australian life-savers volunteer for clubs, pay an annual fee and help raise money through public donations, which the government then matches dollar for dollar to provide equipment. In return, Dirk's perks were that he could sleep in the club house on Magnetic

Island off Townsville for a dollar fifty cents a night and get his meals for one dollar. As he and Susie went off to the bar together, I was delighted to hear Dirk admitting that during the sea-wasp season he had to wear pantihose.

Queensland Railways may be narrow gauge but their carriages are wide enough to lie sideways in with a corridor beyond, and they go slowly enough to be easy to sleep in. Morning tea, biscuits and a 'G'day' arrive at six-thirty. Susie and Dirk weren't at breakfast. Sugarcane fields began in earnest around Ayr where the coastal mountains precipitate sufficient rain. The two-foot gauge railways that cart the cane around in screeching cages, after the fields have been burnt off and harvested, run across roads and scuttle down main streets like those on the west coast of Fiji.

The Sunlander dawdled increasingly on the second day as it entered the Far North. Bored with their compartments, passengers spent most of their time in the lounge car. Some played cards and waited for Townsville, where the Inlander would take them on to the mines at Mount Isa: the younger men tattooed, the older ones brylcreemed, their women short-haired, tight-mouthed and huge, everyone smoking or eating, and baby – there's always a baby – the focus of their attention.

Conspicuously different in this lounge bar were the single women. As well as Susie, there was a girl in her early twenties immersed in a serious paperback; an English-woman who had emigrated to Canberra ten years before and didn't like it, being clearly the sort who wouldn't have been happy anywhere – she was trying *Heart of Darkness* but couldn't find the energy; and there was Corie, of green eyes and surprisingly feminine build for someone who had motorbiked 'eight thousand ks' (kilometres) on her last holiday. As green eyes fascinate me I tried to interest Corie in a discussion as to whether the unofficial title which I had heard an Adelaide lecturer award to Australian women – 'the bearers of culture' – was fair or not.

This academic edited a poetry magazine and had found that eight or nine out of every ten submissions came from women; and it was his impression also that university arts courses in Australia are as dominated by women as science courses are by men. Amongst twentieth-century novelists too, Miles Franklin, H. H. Richardson and Christina Snead have to be considered as illustrious as any three names that Australian men can put forward; and for A. D. Hope's poetry there is Judith Wright's not far behind. Furthermore, as sopranos, novelists, poets and film directors – in the areas where opportunities have existed – Australian women have fully contributed as bearers of culture.

Corie observed, however, how that differed markedly from their role in the administration of the arts or indeed of anything else: no woman professor at Melbourne until the mid-1970s, then a great furore over her appointment, and still no more than a handful around the country even now. As for politicians, there had been no more than seventeen women in the Senate and only six in the House of Representatives from the turn of the century until the 1983 elections.

Peter was in the lounge bar too – in fact he was in the lounge bar whenever he could escape from his wife. I kept meeting him later in Cairns and Kuranda, and Peter was fun, when he wasn't with his wife. He was an American, born in the Ukraine and working for the United Nations, who drank like an Aussie. He had been posted to the Maldives and had visited South Africa, where he found the jokes to be remarkably similar to the ones in Queensland: like, a white driver knocks down a native, and the first question a policeman asks is if the car's all right. Or there's this American television crew that comes to town to film a show in the 'That's Incredible' series – and they find one Abo who is sober and another who's working.

That evening, when the Sunlander was an hour late in reaching Cairns, Peter remarked that the coast to the north of Cairns was Marvin country – because that was where Lee Marlin went fishing. I'd had enough by then. I checked into a hotel by the sluggish waters along the front and tried to convince Corie that she personally was a bearer of culture.

Clarrie's story was that he had been an Australian light-heavyweight champion during the fifties and made eleven thousand pounds out of boxing, had invested it all in a timber business, and had gone magnificently broke in the sixties. Between bouts and bankruptcies he had fathered no fewer than thirty-eight children, who were now spread over the continent between Cairns and Alice Springs; and of this Old Testament-style progeny he said not quite one-third were legitimate. But he didn't give me the impression that he was 'blowing', either about his powers of boxing or begetting. He was after all a potent mixture: half-Irish, half-Aborigine.

Yarrabah is an hour's drive south of Cairns, as Surfers Paradise is from Brisbane. At the time old Clarrie took me there it was one of nineteen Aboriginal reserves on the mainland of Queensland that contained half the state's population of Aborigines, estimated at 60,000. As Clarrie was an hour and a half late turning up one morning to drive me, I waited and looked at the posters in support of Namibia and the Palestinians which tend to line the walls of Aboriginal offices nowadays, though it is only recently that Aborigines have started to join such international protest movements. But how can you be annoyed with an old libertine for being late, when he laughs so infectiously, stops by the road to pick a fig-leaf and plays 'Down the way where the nights are gay' upon his leaf while still keeping both hands on the driving wheel?

Though the distance by sea is only eight miles from Cairns to Yarrabah, it took us an hour's drive because of the rough road winding past mangrove swamps and cane fields, and because of frequent stops for Clarrie to pick up fresh fig-leaves or old offspring. Eventually we stopped on a hill above Yarrabah's main township, tucked around a headland in a bay. Off shore, forty yards from the beach, lay the rusted hulk of a small coastal ship – it had lain there since the Second World War. We looked down at the centre of the township, which was dominated by an area of swamp ground that was being slowly filled in. It didn't look any poorer than an African or West Indian village, but it communicated a greater air of lack of purpose. Nobody was in a hurry to go anywhere, except the incorrigible Clarrie who set off briskly upon our arrival . . . no doubt with a view to his thirty-ninth.

While he was away I was told the story of Yarrabah by one of his uncles. (There are several thousand people on Yarrabah and not one of those I met failed to be one of Clarrie's uncles or nephews or cousins or nieces.) This particular uncle was an Aboriginal police sergeant – 'a Murri copper' – who had recently retired. His name was Mark Noble, and he was indeed one of the most noble men I've met. He had three teeth left, all in one corner of his mouth and they weren't in great shape either, but an immense dignity suffused his presence. By rising to the rank of sergeant he had gone as far up the Aboriginal status ladder as it was possible for him to go. In white terms he had made it, and become part of the force for (white) law and order; so with his age and experience he wasn't going to talk like a red revolutionary about those archaic Queensland laws which incredibly continue to exist in a state that claims to be a democracy. He began by saying, correctly as the law stood, and without bitterness or rancour: 'I and the land I live on are the property of this state. At any time I can be told where I have to live, what work I have to do, whom I'm allowed to see. As for you, you can be thrown off this reserve at any moment for not having a permit.'

Yarrabah was the first Aboriginal mission station in Queensland, established in 1892 according to Noble. The Church of England ran it until the 1960s, with one priest as the sole white man on the reserve. Its inhabitants belonged to two major tribal groups, but sundry Aborigines rounded up in the west of Queensland during the 1920s were sent there as well. Nevertheless, they lived together fairly harmoniously and self-sufficiently. They ran eight farms at Yarrabah that supplied fruit to Cairns; sold some timber; fished around the bay. Reserve members elected their own council, consisting of a representative of each main trade – fisherman, farmer, builder and so forth – and in conjunction with the Anglican priest they ran their own affairs. A price did have to be paid, in return for such independence: everyone went to church – or to the chapel which each farm had – twice a day and thrice on Sundays.

But even old Clarrie, when I asked him later, felt this hadn't done him much harm.

Came the sixties and Yarrabah, like most church missions in Queensland, was taken over by the state government. The Department of Aboriginal and Islander Affairs ('Affairs' being later changed to the more patronising 'Advancement') took control of the reserve. The director of the DAIA, a thousand miles away in Brisbane, became their supreme authority. And this director, appointed by the state government and acting in the name of Her Majesty in London, was invested with far more autocratic powers than Her Majesty or her predecessors had enjoyed since the abolition of the Divine Right of Kings. The Yarrabah Council continued, but its job now was to rubber-stamp whatever had been decided by the director in Brisbane, or by the white manager of each reserve acting in his name. Anything the council decided on the director or manager could overrule, but not of course vice versa; and thus it still was in the Year of Our Lord 1983.

Since this shift in authority, the fabric of life on Yarrabah has been – some would say deliberately – unpicked. The eight farms supplying the entire nutritional needs of the community were reduced to one. Why? Noble was polite enough not to make this sound a naive question: why, as he put it, would local subsistence farming be encouraged after the DAIA had erected a new store on Yarrabah, run by a white man, with all profits going to the DAIA in Brisbane? Even though, quite apart from the unhealthy effect of such changes in diet, the introduction of western canned food was bound to sap the collective will to be self-sufficient, as has been observed in many other cultures.

Significantly, also, there had been no alcohol in mission days. In the sixties, according to Noble, it began appearing in bottles and flagons brought in from Cairns as rapidly as the Aborigines' self-respect and self-sufficiency declined. Then the community was offered a canteen which sold beer (all profits going to the DAIA – which never has to account publicly for what happens to those profits) from five o'clock until nine each evening, and the customers of the beer canteen quickly learnt to use their four limited hours to maximum effect. They would drink wine by the flagon – with methylated spirits for further fuel. And inevitably, without either personal experience of alcohol or traditional social customs for dealing with it, the results were terrible. *In vino veritas*: in 'metho' mutilation. Alcohol in various forms rapidly undid the complex weave of Aboriginal life.

The chief reason why they voted in favour of this canteen, Noble thought, was in order to keep up with the white man. To keep up with the white man . . . He was sitting on a packing-case in the shade while I squatted on the steps leading up to his bare three-room house on stilts. Clearly even a lifetime's employment as a teetotal policeman had left him with little more than the most basic material necessities.

Old Clarrie's car stirred up dust in the road outside and he got out, sweating and pleased with himself. By now the afternoon was so humid and still that mere breaths from the sea failed to stir our droplets of sweat or the palm fronds overhead. Clarrie helped himself to orange juice and perched on a higher step while Mark Noble waited to resume his matter-of-fact discourse. What was most surprising about him, about Clarrie and all Aborigines I met, was their lack of bitterness. Because of this they have never resorted to violence or terrorism, and the world therefore hears very little about Brisbane's discrimination.

The rate of homicide amongst Aborigines on Queensland reserves is high: to be precise, twenty-eight times higher than the rate in the United Kingdom on official figures, which are underestimates so as not to cause embarrassment to the Queensland government. The pattern behind these killings is consistently the same: most Aborigines who commit homicide live on reserves, often transported there from their tribal homeland; alcohol is drunk by them in prodigious quantities; no strangers or white people are the victims, only the killer's close family and friends; and he normally has no idea of what he has done until he wakes up the next morning and finds the body of his victim. Attempts at suicide and self-mutilation are also many times higher than the national average; and women too are taking increasingly to excessive drinking and to carving up their loved ones. All of which is a direct consequence, says a Queensland University sociologist, of 'Europeanisation'. Given western alcohol, knives and guns, and deprived of their native homelands and control over their own affairs, Aborigines take their frustration out on each other – not on those who have ultimately caused it.

In Yarrabah, which had previously been self-sufficient, the DAIA sent in white plumbers, white carpenters, white policemen and white farming supervisors to cultivate special cash-crops (profits going of course to the DAIA). These employees are given free accommodation, free electricity, help with transport, and salaries four times what an Aborigine is paid for doing what is sometimes the same work. With these arrangements the DAIA in Brisbane could proclaim to the outside world that the Queensland government has generously spent two hundred and thirty-three million dollars from 1970 to 1980 under the heading of Aboriginal welfare, figures which its apologists gleefully promulgate. At the same time it refused to pay Aboriginal reserve members the state's legal minimum wage.

In return for receiving the help of these white supervisors (I watched one of them standing beside a house while his Murri assistants put the roof on), Yarrabah members pay rent of between ten and thirty dollars a week for the shanty housing which the DAIA allots them, and are given the privilege of subsidising the white-consumed electricity. Average pay is the sixty dollars a week which most of them receive as dole (paid by the federal government in Canberra, which has always been more humane). If one wonders why half Queensland Aborigines tolerate living on reserves, here we have the answer: there isn't much change out of sixty dollars a week to cover the fifty-thousand-dollar mortgage needed for a home outside.

Needless to say, amongst the other features of reserve life which Brisbane propaganda doesn't mention, white policemen have the power to arrest anyone on a reserve, while Aboriginal policemen can only touch their own kind. Medical facilities? Adequate to make the death rate from infectious diseases amongst Aborigines on reserves ninety times higher than the state average. Education facilities? Only the day before Clarrie took me to see the reserve's school consisting of two pre-fab buildings deposited in a car park, the Member for Cairns, Ray Jones, had paid a visit and remarked: 'There isn't a school in Queensland like it where there is such a lack of facilities.'

That evening Clarrie drove happily back to Cairns for a plate of steak and eggs, but I couldn't join him in his fig-leaf whistling. Why hadn't all the petty bureaucratic discriminations of the Queensland government quenched his vitality, or soured Noble's spirit? I wondered what the residents of Surfers Paradise would think of regulations like: 'All able-bodied persons over the age of fifteen years residing within the Community/Reserve shall, unless otherwise determined by the Manager, perform such work as directed by the Manager, Council or persons authorised by him.' Or how would they react to a rule such as: 'A person shall not use any electrical goods whatsoever, other than electric light, during certain hours declared by the Council or Manager as prohibited hours for use of such electrical equipment.' Or pettier still: 'A birthday party may be consented to by the Council with approval from the immediate neighbours.'

An emotive word is genocide, but it so happens that Australia – on behalf of the state of Queensland – ratified the Genocide Convention of 1949, which specified that crimes under international law include:

> causing serious bodily or mental harm to members of the group (that is, a national, ethnic, racial or religious minority)
> deliberately inflicting on the group conditions of life calculated to bring about its physical destruction in whole or in part.

Have these conditions of life been created on the reserves of Queensland? Old Clarrie may not have demeaned himself by becoming bitter or vengeful, but he knows the answer.

11

Cairns to Forsayth

The creeks run dry
Or ten feet high
And it's either drought
Or plenty

(Anon)

The 19.30 Mixed Goods from Cairns to Forsayth every Monday, which as everyone knows stops at Redlynch, Stoney Creek, Kuranda, Koah, Biboohra, Mareeba, Dimbulah, Verdure, Lappa, Alma-den, Gelaro, Bullock Creek, Lyndbrook, Fossilbrook Creek, Frewhurst, Mount Surprise, Einasleigh, Wirra-Wirra (provided you ask the guard) and Forsayth, is not quite like any other train in Australia – unless it is the 22.10 Mixed Goods from Cairns to Forsayth every Wednesday, which also stops at Redlynch, Stoney Creek, Kuranda, etc.

Entering one of the two antique carriages at the rear of the Mixed Goods, a passenger (there is seldom more than one) is in a strange kind of way taking his seat for a seven-thirty concert. The music however is neither orchestral nor the euphonious puff of steam and the lonesome whistle, nor even the throb of diesel backed by cicadas in the cane fields outside. The train's wheels play this symphony. As they round the first of the many corners that wind up the mountainside to Kuranda, one wheel sounds a groaning note; another takes up the cry, higher-pitched; nocturnal silence follows until the train rounds a still sharper curve and another wheel lets out a scream into the valley below. Then yet another wheel grinds, others shriek, until the whole train takes up the cacophony, shrilling, shrieking into the night. It could be the Symphony of

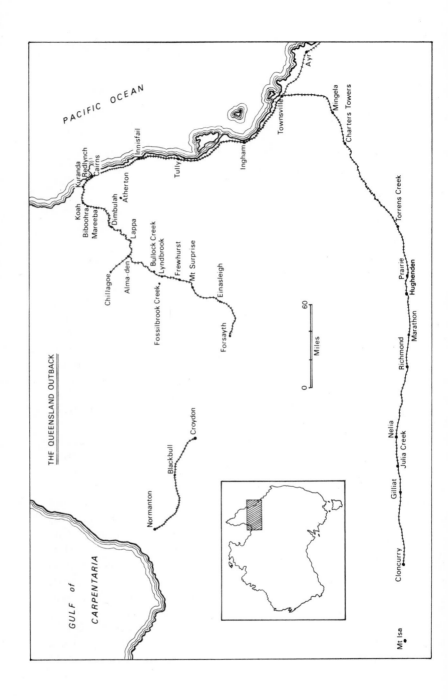

THE QUEENSLAND OUTBACK

Screams, lasting an eerie hour until Kuranda is reached and the plateau of the Atherton Tableland.

Rainforest – which has been ninety-nine per cent destroyed in the rest of Australia – and babbling waterfalls make the ride up from Cairns to Kuranda the most scenic rail journey in the country. And a few years ago the rampant, luxuriant, even decadent growth also made Kuranda an ideal setting for the hippy capital of Australia. It's no longer hippy: though it still pursues alternative lifestyles, Kuranda has 'upped its game', as one local phrased it. An ashram offers video courses on yoga and meditation; a two-day seminar on Dianetics is yours for fifty dollars ('bring a bag lunch, paper, pens and a copy of *Dianetics, the Modern Science of Mental Health* by Ron Hubbard'). There's a French restaurant in the main street and health food shops *ad nauseam*, one of them selling marshmallow hand cream and, for undisclosed purposes, Swami Sarasvati's avocado night cream (with vitamin E).

Vestiges of hippyism remain in Kuranda's open-air Sunday market. The few disciples going gently to seed in the bush come to town then in sarongs – no bras – and sandals to sell their organically grown vegetables and homemade coconut cake. But there aren't many of them left. A bearded potter reckoned that most of those who had arrived on the hippy trail to Kuranda in the late sixties and early seventies had gone back to Sydney and Melbourne to be accountants.

So it took a bit of searching before I came across a survivor of that bizarre episode in Queensland's modern history known as 'the Bay of Pigs'. This police operation by land, sea and air was launched in August 1976 to seek out and destroy a colony of fifty to sixty hippies who were living on the coast around Cooktown, in that area which Edmund Kennedy found so impenetrable.

Martin, dark and short-haired, was still no more than early twenties. Not a hippy himself, he nevertheless offered a version which differed significantly from those official accounts which at the time sent an embarrassed titter around the rest of more liberal Australia: 'When I first went to Cedar Bay there were about ten people. I went along with a fisherman who knew it and wanted to take his wife

179

and kids with him.' Martin was propped on a bar-stool in a most agreeable hotel thirty yards from Kuranda station. 'We decided it was a bloody good place to live. We hunted the turkeys and the pigs that had run wild, and old Bill didn't charge us anything to live there.

'Old Bill, he was a sort of hermit. He'd been a miner and he still held a mining lease at the north end of Cedar Bay. Then some hippies moved in – vegetarians most of 'em growing a bit of grass – to the south end of the bay. This was National Park land and we had no right to go there, chopping down trees and stuff. We were doing the wrong thing all right, but the police could have been a bit more subtle about it.'

They were subtle to the extent that one Friday evening policemen were called in from all over the FNQ to Cairns HQ. The next day they spent going to the same department store in large groups and equipping themselves with clothes and equipment suitable for bush warfare, so that by Saturday evening everyone in Cairns had guessed that a police raid was imminent, with Cedar Bay the likely target. But it was impossible for anyone to pass on warning of this impending raid, since even today telephones do not exist, the only normal way of reaching Cedar Bay is by walking four hours along the beach at low tide, it has no electricity, gas or road, and it lost its nearest contact with the outside world when the Cooktown–Cairns railway was closed for lack of custom in 1962.

At dawn on Sunday morning the force went in, attacking by land and sea, with aerial support. From the navy patrol boat *Bayonet* and the anti-narcotics vessel *Jabiru* thirty-six men stormed ashore. As Martin remembers it: 'They arrived in dinghies with hand guns and automatics, shooting down the pawpaws, handcuffing a few people, chopping up the irrigation hoses with machetes, stampeding over the gardens – the usual stuff when they do a bloody raid. About four of us hit the bush when we saw the boats coming – we didn't have time to warn everyone else and left 'em on the beach.'

Those captured were herded together and made to sit back-to-back on the beach, women and children included.

The more insidious-looking of these terrorists were wound up in fish nets. Five dwellings were doused in kerosene and with their contents set alight. A Cessna wheeled overhead to spot any fugitives, and a helicopter from Cairns brought in chief inspector Robert Gray to mastermind the follow-up to this assault.

Did the police go slightly over the top? The outcome of this raid was that four people were charged in Cooktown court with possessing cannabis and eight with vagrancy. Thirty thousand dollars were spent on bringing these desperadoes to justice, as a result of which two were jailed for possessing cannabis, the others fined.

Gray, the Cairns police chief, was far from repentant afterwards. He stood by all these official details and went on to declare: 'As an exercise the raid was particularly successful. We look forward to more successful ventures of this type in the future . . . We left a big group of these hippies still living at Cedar Bay. A lot of them fled like stirred-up meat ants when we moved in.'

Queensland's police minister at the time was Tom Newbery, one of the Bjelke-Petersen 'ten'. He justified the action in the following vivid terms: 'The stench of human excrement was overpowering and the rotting carcasses of two wild pigs lay near a sluggish creek which served as a water supply.' But it was for another reason, because of the heavy-handedness of his boys in blue, that this raid came to be known as 'The Bay of Pigs'. And it was after this affair blew up that the police commissioner Whitrod resigned, saying there were signs that Queensland was becoming a police state.

The Mixed Goods to Forsayth takes twenty-two and a half hours for its journey of 423 kilometres, supposing it's punctual, which works out at an average speed barely above ten mph. However a delay meant more time on my journey was lost at Mareeba: the guard announced at midnight that something was wrong with one of the carriages and it had to be detached. So everyone piled into the second-class carriage, which had benches running down either side and a door at each end. Each of these doors opened on to a platform, like an old Casey Jones caboose. One of the advantages of the Mixed Goods from Cairns is that it never goes fast enough for it to be dangerous to sit on these platforms, dangle one's feet and watch the bush go by.

Three Thursday Islanders in shrouds took up most of the carriage. Nobody touched them or told them to budge over, mate. An Italian grasping a package climbed in and sat upright between two of them for the rest of the night with sad, gleaming eyes – the ghost of Varischetti. Feeling thirsty I took a drink from the plastic carafe in one dusty corner that was labelled QR, discovered it must have stood for Quite Revolting and lay down in the vacant bench space. My choice was between suffocation inside and mosquitoes outside. Since nothing is more hateful on earth than the mosquitoes' whine I wrapped a shirt around my head and chose suffocation. Stupor followed and in the long hours when resistance is lowest, I had to attempt positive thinking: like, not 'Oh, mossies!', but thinking of Susie – 'Oh, mmm, Aussies!'

We make fun of those we love: the Mixed Goods to Forsayth is my favourite Australian train. Not that I would go on it again for the sake of enjoying what Cicero calls 'the familiar comforts': it offers no food or buffet car or even water, unless you risk the QR carafe or – no less dangerous – disturb a sleeping Thursday Islander to ask for a swig from his water-bag. The pleasure of the Mixed Goods is that it offers a taste of old Australia. The Mixed Goods from Cairns to Forsayth is a throwback to the days of Laurie O'Byrne, shovelling coal on his pioneer track and chasing 'roos with his poker; an echo of the old Ghan winding its way around and sometimes through the tributaries of Lake Eyre, to arrive in Alice Springs a day late, or a week, or two or three.

The shunting of mosquitoes finally allowed me some sleep; whereupon one of the wooden guillotine-type shutters banged down in the window above my head. In the grey pre-dawn light the FNQ landscape was strangely familiar, but not until we had rolled along for a while further did it click that we were now in the same latitude as Pine Creek country. The scrubby hillocks, some burnt out, and the russet man-sized anthills were the same, as were the frequent feather-boas of pandanus. And there was the same mysterious stamp upon the land: man might never have existed in these parts, no impression had he left, except for this railway.

We were on another line leading to nowhere, Alma-den being an upmarket version of nowhere, simply the place where the line divides for Chillagoe to the south and Forsayth to the east. Still, you can get an excellent breakfast in the pub at Alma-den. As the sun and the smell of bacon rose, and dew dripped, chickens ranged freely beyond the verandah in what was either the pub's backyard or else the main street of Alma-den. Fifty people live there, according to the publican's wife, every man employed by Queensland Railways, and they keep going by waiting for each cattle-mustering season. The trains were designed to run out to Chillagoe when it was a copper mine, and Forsayth when it was a goldfield, but that was sixty years ago and the line hasn't had any mineral traffic for over half a century.

When the publican's wife brought in breakfast she almost dropped the plate of bacon and eggs at the sight of the day-old newspaper I was reading. A day-old newspaper in Alma-den terms is in mint condition, still hot from the lead type of the press. They don't have television of course in Alma-den; just three trains a week in each direction, and quite a few flies.

For the rest of the day the Mixed Goods went bush-whacking along, every hour or so reaching some kind of settlement, albeit just an uninhabited hut or a siding with a ramp from which to load cattle: places that exist only by reason of some Lewis Carroll kind of logic. I asked one railwayman why Forsayth (population seventy) existed and he replied 'because of the railway'; and, contrariwise, the railway in turn exists because of Forsayth. Nobody in their right mind would build a line there now, but since one is there already nobody has the heart to stop it.

Bullock Creek was one such settlement: a creek with no bullock, let alone a human being. Insects were strewn over the top of its muddy water – not the sort of billabong in which Jenny Agutter swam naked in *Walkabout*. A stockyard, a ramp and rusty siding were the suggestions of human life.

Lyndbrook. *Lyndbrook*? The name befitting a country house in London's leafy stockbroker belt looked incongruous here. The station was made up of a tin hut, no platform and a sign saying 'Ladies', plural. I had not seen a lady, singular, in the three hours since Alma-den.

Varischetti departed about noon at a siding which had no name and two carriages converted into sleeping quarters. After sitting upright all night on the Mixed Goods, he looked as if he had been trapped underground for at least ten days. Only the three Thursday Islanders remained, their long thin heads poking out from the shrouds. 'TIs', for short, are famous for their role in building railways, the 'GIs' of the permanent way. They have developed a reputation the Irish would envy for working tremendously hard and drinking harder. When these three emerged after sleeping it off, one of them told me they lived in Cairns, spent a fortnight working on track maintenance for ten hours a day then returned by Mixed Goods to Cairns for four days off.

I couldn't catch everything Willie Flinders said but when a flock of black cockatoos flew overhead he commented: 'Lot of wild life out here.' Yet the publican's wife in Alma-den had maintained that there was nothing out here, and so far that morning I'd seen one wallaby, one scrub bull and a sign saying 'Ladies': my inexperienced eyes must have merely looked while Willie's had seen. He went on to express himself delighted at the amount of water in Fossilbrook Creek after a localised overnight shower: he said he would be motoring down the track on a section car after work to go fishing for bream. And would he swim? Willie widened his eyes. No, he wasn't going to swim: he didn't believe the official story that the freshwater crocodiles which lurk around the Gulf country don't bite humans.

When the TI trio climbed down at Frewhurst – another leafy suburban name for six tin shacks – Willie's mates were lying on mattresses outside. One spoke for all when he shouted from his mattress: 'Hurry up, Willie, we're rarin' to go!' All teeth flashed in smiles. But although this fettlers' gang of Thursday Islanders were in placid, even jovial mood, I doubt whether Mrs Aeneas Gunn would have risked pelting them with bits of her melon peel.

At Mount Surprise the train lay for an hour around noon while the wind of the desert blew over it. Flies buzzed; as in Adlestrop no one left and no one came. Mount Surprise, what there is of it, is run by a station-mistress who wanted to know why I was going to Forsayth by train and not by bus, which was much quicker. 'When's the bus?' I asked. 'On Thursdays,' she said helpfully. It was Tuesday.

The guard (the only other person on the Mixed Goods by now apart from its driver) came up and offered his copy of the *Queensland Country Lines Timetable* to while away the time of shunting. He said it was 'good readin'' – such good reading that it had taken the place of the old *Bulletin* as the major item on many a bushman's shelf. It has some of the arcane detail of an old Bradshaw's, listing the stations with 'Rooms and Tea Stalls Conducted by Private Individuals'. After an hour at Mount Surprise I felt up to a Mastermind examination on the thirteen Queensland Stations possessing Licensed Rooms (including Kuranda), with special reference to those with Temperance Rooms (Bogantungan and Sandgate).

Classification of Parcels also makes for 'good readin'': one learns that 'birds, stuffed (in cases)' have to be transported on Queensland Railways at double the normal rate; so do canoes, in addition to go-karts and wire rat-traps. All these go at double rate, which seems fair and reasonable. But in that case why should 'grass (pampas and Kikuyu)' or orchids be allowed to travel at the ordinary rate? And why on earth should 'ghee [de-hydrated butter] packed in cans or wrapped in foil' be allowed to go at half fare, when ghee in mid-summer after two days on the Mixed Goods, whether or not it is wrapped in foil, is going to be considerably more lethal than any rat-trap? PS 'Prior arrangements must be made for the conveyance of corpses by rail. The rate for each corpse will be twenty cents per kilometre, minimum charge eleven dollars.'

Thereafter, on the next stretch to Einasleigh, more pale green sameness and light brown nothing. Later some cattle added themselves to the landscape, a few of them skeletons beside the track but most of them alive and ruminating. The breed found to be most suited to the Gulf Country is the legendarily hardy Droughtmaster, five-eighths Indian Brahman. Its hardiness was being tested. 'How are you going?' the station-mistress at Mount Surprise had asked of a grazier. 'Oh, she'll be all right – if it rains for the next month.' Anthills in the scrub were now as fired clay. Stony rubbish all around, and no cooling breeze to be had on the carriage platform. When the wind itself is hot, life cannot have long to go.

At Mount Surprise our large diesel locomotive had been replaced with two smaller ones, light enough for the line through to Forsayth – this stretch of track was pure pioneer stuff, following the contours, never bothering with bridge or culvert. Hereabouts the train was down to two diesels, seven wagons, the second-class carriage, a guard's van and a QR living quarters carriage. But little though the trains carry outside the cattle season, at least they carry it at forty dollars a ton, compared with the seventy dollars on the monster lorries known as road-trains.

So primitive is this track that even when doing no more than twenty mph the Mixed Goods feels as though it's belting along. And you watch the passing scene, staring from the shaded carriage platform, anxious as always on a new journey not to miss some unusual feature: waiting for a stream, an animal, a person, some trace of man's existence which will enable you to turn away, satisfied at having spotted something different. But nothing comes along to break the spell, nothing that an untrained white eye could detect. Just trees: millions of them, trillions of trees, every one a drought-blasted gum. 'Hail friendly tree!' say Europe's poets; but these of the bush are more impersonal. Indeed it struck me that this might be limbo, where lost souls are sent and immortalised, each as a ghost gum tree.

Slowly the sun had mercy. As it sank, it lit up the bush. It could have been a Hans Heysen sunset – that wonderfully golden painting of his that portrays a bullock team and drovers plodding their weary way o'er a South Australian lea, and not a fly or mosquito in sight. But then there seems often to have been this rose-tinted view of the Australian bush. The Swiss émigré, Louis Buvelot, painted dreamy Corot landscapes of mid-nineteenth-century Australia, complete with dale, bole and sun-kissed rill: you feel he was itching to put a Roman temple in the place of yon humble homestead. It took a century of settlement before the Heidelberg School, led by Streeton and McCubbin, could see the bush as it was through native eyes, not romantic European ones – to be followed by Nolan and Drysdale.

More recently, Australian film producers have cashed in on this rosy conception of the bush: with brilliant camera-work, and a vitality that is refreshing after stale Hollywood, they have portrayed a succession of camps at sunset, horses flicking their tails and faithful Abo stockmen saying, 'Yes, boss.' *The Man From Snowy River*, for a start . . .

A more realistic view of the bush was propounded by that unique literary figure in the Anglo-Saxon world, Henry Lawson. Kipling and Hardy and numerous others have written about the masses – soldiers in the ranks, peasant farmers – but Lawson alone is said to have been a writer both *of* the people and *for* the people. (One would have hoped Australia would produce this phenomenon, to prove that the legend of egalitarianism has substance.)

Railways played quite a part in Lawson's life – not a happy one, but then no part of the life of Australia's finest early writer appears to have been particularly happy. Born in 1867, he grew up in central New South Wales and learnt the Irish folk tunes and old border ballads that were still being sung on the goldfields. Apart from one long visit to Bourke by train he never went back to the bush after his teens, which allowed the critics to allege that he did not fully know what he was writing about; but he had probably experienced enough at an impressionable age.

Moving to Sydney with his mother, Lawson lived in a

rented cottage of four rooms, two of them sub-let, and found such a rate of unemployment that he knew what it was like to go down to the newspaper offices at four o'clock in the morning to catch the 'Jobs Vacant' column in the first editions. Eventually he got a job at Hudson Brothers' railway carriage works in the suburb of Clyde and settled into a routine of rising at five, walking to Redfern Station and catching the workmen's train at six o'clock. He saw on his way 'the wretched rag-covered forms on the benches, and under them, and on the grass'. On the train 'there was a nasty guard who always woke me up about Homebush to look at my workman's ticket'. At work he had to prime the carriage surfaces, while mocked on occasion for being a bit deaf and strange; Australia has never loved the non-conformer. In the evenings he returned to Redfern and got home about six-thirty, too tired to continue his self-education.

Nevertheless, he began to write, and at the age of twenty-one he had his first, and maybe best-known poem published in *The Bulletin* magazine. Unfortunately, the rest of Lawson's verse did not progress much beyond its initial promise. As might have been expected of a young, ill-educated author, he presents the oppressed condition of the masses with an indignation that is fine and noble, but his ideas for reform are limited to vision of the ranks of the 'Red Revolution' marching to the rescue. It was his short stories of outback Australian life which developed him into a great figure: more poetic than his actual verse, stories like 'Send Round the Hat' or 'The Drover's Wife' capture pathos without being sentimental.

Given his childhood and close acquaintance with the realities of gutter life, Lawson was unlikely to wax lyrical about the bush. No rose-tinted spectacles for him. He knew it as:

Barren ridges, gullies, ridges! where the ever-lasting
  flies
Fiercer than the plagues of Egypt – swarm about your
  blighted eyes!

Or as he once wrote in prose: 'I might be biased – having been there; but it is time the general public knew the back country as it is, if only for the sake of the bush outcasts who have to tramp for ever through broiling mulga scrub and baking lignum.'

Yet even so, there was a romantic enough streak in Lawson for him to have been amongst other nineteenth-century figures in seeing the coming of the Iron Horse as a blow to traditional life. He wasn't of the purblind Duke of Wellington type when it came to trains ('I see no reason to suppose that these machines will ever force themselves into general use'); but like Tolstoy and Hardy he wondered if material progress was worth the destruction of old rustic ways – no more drays and bullocks and golden-dusted Heysen scenes. He summed up his ambivalence in the first and last verses of 'The Roaring Days':

The night too quickly passes
    And we are growing old,
So let us fill our glasses
    And toast the Days of Gold;
When finds of wondrous treasure
    Set all the South ablaze,
And you and I were faithful mates
    All through the Roaring Days!

Those golden days are vanished,
    And altered is the scene;
The diggings are deserted,
    The camping-grounds are green,
The flaunting flag of progress
    Is in the West unfurled,
The mighty Bush with iron rails
    Is tethered to the world.

The sun had gone by the time we at last wound along the bank of a tree-lined creek down towards Forsayth, and at seven o'clock, just an hour late, the Mixed Goods terminated in an empty expanse. From its carriage platform I walked the hundred yards up to the buffers and looked back. From Forsayth in deepest Queensland the iron rails stretched to Alma-den, where the publican's wife would then have been cooking steaks for tea, to Kuranda and Cairns, where old Clarrie was no doubt lining up his evening's entertainment; from Cairns to Brisbane, from Brisbane to Sydney, where commuters were finishing their journey home; from Sydney over to Adelaide and across to Cook, where the rails would still have been burning hot, to the Kalgoorlie discovered by Paddy Hannan, and finally to Perth on the shore of the Indian Ocean, tethering the mighty bush to the world for heaven knows how many thousands of miles.

12

Croydon to Normanton

'I know it's a joke to a lot of people. They find I'm Officer-in-Charge of a line that's as crooked as a dog's hind leg and hidden in lush seasons with waist high grass and serving only a couple of hundred people over its whole length. They don't see anything more than that. And I'm too busy to tell them.'
(Stan Tuesley, formerly of the Croydon–Normanton line, to Patsy Adam Smith)

The eight-thirty a.m. from Croydon in western Queensland is not as trains are from Surrey's Croydon. No one paces the platform with bowler hat and rolled umbrella, or folds his morning newspaper and attempts the back-page cross-word. When the train is late, no one resigns himself to delay with silent phlegmatism and tugs his raincoat around him for extra warmth.

For a start, there is only one train a week from the Queensland Croydon, at eight-thirty every Thursday morning; and there is no platform to pace. Besides, anyone wearing a bowler hat in the region around the Gulf of Carpentaria would be reckoned a 'woofter' or English, probably both. And should someone waiting for the train's departure happen to be doing a crossword, it will be one in a two-day old edition of *The Cairns Post*.

On the ant-strewn strip of concrete serving as a platform all the passengers squatted together that Thursday morning: three Aboriginal full-bloods with swags and rucksacks beside them. This Croydon station has no buffet to be open, or closed without explanation, nor a waiting-room nor bookstall. But it can boast a Gents and Ladies, they being one and the same contrivance – a corrugated-iron shack containing a thunderbox with wooden seat.

In the station's only other building both the Fahrenheit and flies had already passed the hundred mark. This tin hut is what remained after a cyclone struck Croydon in 1974, with a roof stuck on top of the leftovers (such is the old Australian ability to improvise). And on the rails outside, waiting to depart, stood a living railway fossil, the train buff's equivalent of a coelacanth.

Then, as eight-thirty approached, there assembled inside this building the Croydon station-master and the Normanton station-master, the train driver and the pay clerk, the chief mechanic of the Normanton–Croydon Railway and the maintenance supervisor, together with the station-masters of the intervening halts at Blackbull, Haydon, Glenore and Clarina. It might be thought, therefore, that the tin hut was bursting at its seams. But in fact only the single chair in it was occupied – for Mr Honey, as Officer-in-charge of the whole line, holds all these positions.

His second-in-command – indeed his sole assistant in running eighty-four miles of railway – is Paddy the porter, who was loading a few parcels outside. But Paddy too is not like the porters at the other Croydon (so one would imagine), being a long-haired Aborigine in a light blue bath-towel cap.

For company Mr Honey had in his hut a pair of boots, a fan, a television displaying the test card, a broom and one of those telephones the handle of which you have to turn to make a call. Croydon has long been promised satellites and microwave-links by the politicians in Brisbane, but for the moment you have to wind the handle and ask the operator to put you through to a number in the outside world, or even in Croydon. To complete the inventory of Mr Honey's equipment, there was a list of the six telephone numbers considered essential to the running of his line.

Mr Honey himself had that Andy Capp knack of being able to talk without letting an own-rolled cigarette fall from his nether lip. His head was half-bald, or as he may prefer to see it, half-covered with dark hair. In spite of his numerous responsibilities, he was able to find time to push back his felt hat, wave his hand at a fly in the Aussie salute and speak about the duties involved in running one train per week in each direction.

'On Mondays there's repairin' and servicin'. On Tuesdays there's servicin' and repairin', plus I do the invoicin' and get the train together. Wednesdays I drive it here in the morning and do the paperwork this end. Thursdays I drive it back to Normanton and pay the staff cheques. Fridays, well . . .' Mr Honey was then one year into his four-year posting as Officer-in-charge beside the Gulf of Carpentaria, and he let it be known that he had to pace himself in the heat.

'There's six blackfellas too, as a fettlers' gang. There used to be five of them fixin' the track with a white fella, and for the month he was with them they did more work than in the previous seven years. They thought he was an inspector!' (There was also a woman in Croydon who complained that she always saw these fettlers leaning on their shovels whenever the train passed – as if they would mend the track when the train was passing.) 'And there's Paddy the porter,' Mr Honey added with a grunt.

He looked at the Croydon station clock; then closed its case with a click and put it back in his pocket. He glanced up the station road to see if any more passengers were coming. No double-decker buses and rows of semi-detached – just a dirt track of reddish dust and a single house perched on stilts, with a banger on blocks out the front. A few hundred yards away across the scrub was the lone Croydon pub, not yet open. Statistically, it was unlikely that many more passengers would be coming since the whole shire of Croydon – 10,600 square miles in area, the size of Wales – has a total population of 300 people.

And yet this dot on the map of the Never-Never Land, where men are scarce (and women scarcer still) and only the anthills are prolific, was once a gold-rush town with 30,000 people in its neighbourhood. They came in the 1880s to dig an estimated 50,000 mine shafts in the vicinity – and forgot to cover up most of them afterwards, so that not a few bodies have ended up at the bottom of a shaft.

At the end of the last century this same Croydon on a Saturday night was packed with promenaders beneath gaslights and the Southern Cross, frequenting shops or barbers or its four dozen pubs. In the December of 1887, the year its rush began, there were – so Warden Towner reported – '2,000 miners, 1,500 timber getters, attendants and labourers, 1,500 storekeepers, tradesmen and clerks, 1,000 women and children, and 500 Chinese, Malays, Singalese, and Africans'.

Shops were stocked with merchandise brought from Britain or 'the South' (Sydney and Melbourne) to Thursday Island off Cape York, transhipped up the Norman River to Normanton, and carried from there to Croydon on the remarkable railway. There were local mandarins too for sale in those days, water melons, custard apples and lemons, grown in market-gardens by Chinese balancing water buckets on each end of a pole. These pig-tailed 'Celestials', as they were politely known, made the semi-desert bloom with their intensive cultivation, though no permanent surface water was to be found within twenty miles of Croydon.

Mark Twain might have had Queensland's Croydon specifically in mind when he wrote in *More Tramps Abroad*:

> Australian history is almost always picturesque, indeed, it is so curious and strange, that it is itself the chiefest novelty the country has to offer, and so it pushes the other novelties into second and third place. It does not read like history, but like the most beautiful lies, and all of a fresh sort, no mouldy old stale ones. It is full of surprises and adventures, and incongruities, and contradictions and incredibilities; but they are all true, they all happened.

Twain is right: in Croydon today it feels incongruous, even incredible, that less than a century ago this one-pub town could have been a thousand times more populous.

Yet thus it was – until the mines gave out, the Great War came, and the men left and the shafts were flooded. Cyclone, fire and the irresistible bush completed nature's return. Croydon's streets now are not only not paved with gold, few have bitumen either.

It was nearing eight twenty-five so Mr Honey, having sold four tickets in one of his manifold capacities, and without dropping the cigarette from his mouth, climbed into the front seat of his antique rail motor. Paddy filled the radiator – just like a car radiator – from a water-bag while Mr Honey put his gear-stick into neutral, pulled the choke, pressed the starter, and revved a cloud of fumes through the exhaust pipe outside his door. Then he pressed his right foot on the clutch, wrestled his gear-stick into first, sounded a quick horn blast and with his right hand pushed down on the accelerator lever.

Immediately, as the train surged forwards, lurched sideways and leapt across the points, another exceptional feature of this railway could be appreciated. As its passengers' nerves should be, the track is made entirely of steel and it hasn't been replaced since it was completed in 1891. Steel sleepers and rails do not make for a comfortable ride (the Croydon line indeed might as well be called 'the permanent sway'). But they are a match for Queensland's white ants.

A bushman in the Croydon pub had said, quite soberly, that he had once left a plank on the ground, returned three weeks later and put his finger straight through it: the paint alone had not been eaten. So since conventional wooden sleepers were not going to be practical in this terrain George Phillips, the first line engineer, bethought himself of an alternative and when he came up with one he patented it.

Steel sleepers had been tried before in Queensland, unsuccessfully, and as early as 1855 on the Bristol and Exeter Railway. But the Phillips idea was a variation on this theme: his sleepers were U-shaped and this hollow U-shaped part had first to be filled with mud. They were then turned upside down and laid directly on the ground without any of the usual ballast as a foundation. Packed with mud they weighed three times the forty-five kilogrammes of timber sleepers and were therefore stable enough as they were. They were also cheap, flood-proof and anti-ant.

The Toowoomba Foundry produced some of Phillips's sleepers while the rest came from Glasgow. He had steel rails attached to them with clips, and a train finally rolled over the lot to press it into the ground, leaving the rails a few inches above the scrub. And there they remain, if not exactly in their original position.

During the subsequent decades under Queensland's tropical sun this track has naturally been subjected to considerable heat which has tended to warp it in places. But because these steel rails are firmly anchored to the sleepers and always zig-zag and warp in the same direction – instead of each rail warping outward as can occur with wooden sleepers – they never let the train wheels fall in between them.

The vegetation, however, remains a problem for it grows so high between the rails that only the rails themselves make the track distinguishable from the surrounding scrub. In the wet season, when it rains properly, the grass grows so lushly that cattle hide in it to avoid the bog on either side of the track and the driver has to keep one hand constantly on the horn (of his rail motor, that is).

Above the engine, on a kind of bonnet beside the driver, a brass plate reads: 'Maximum speed of car – forty miles per hour', and I suspect that Mr Honey has the ambition to touch that speed limit on some occasion during his four-year posting. But at first galahs and cockatoos flew past, quietly overtaking, as we left behind the few buildings that are Croydon. Then Mr Honey wrestled into fourth gear and we fairly leapt along.

Passengers in the previous rail motor were warned not to let their hands slip between their seat and the wall because the swaying from side to side could crush their fingers. That was Rail Motor 74, built in 1934, which was much loved in spite of its inherent dangers and served the Croydon line from 1964 to 1982. When this dear old bus was finally taken for repair to the Ipswich workshops outside Brisbane, it was found to be far too old for renovation.

The present one is RM93, built in 1950 to carry twenty-six passengers. It arrived in Normanton in November 1982 after spending its preceding ten years as an inspection car in Rockhampton, and it's taking time to work its way into the affections of those who knew its predecessor but will doubtless do so eventually. RM93 was the second last of its type ever built in Queensland.

As we leapt along I tried to read the timetable without being sea-sick. It reads:

Altitude in Metres	Kilometres from Normanton	Stations	Rail Car Wed Only	Stations	Rail Car Thur Only
12	–	Normanton	dep 0830	Croydon	dep 0830
6	17	Clarina	dep 0905	Blackbull	dep 1030
8	22	Glenore	dep 0915	Haydon	dep 1155
31	62	Haydon	dep 1030	Glenore	dep 1245
53	91	Blackbull	dep 1130	Clarina	dep 1255
112	152	Croydon	arr 1330	Normanton	arr 1330

However, we reached Blackbull – a siding and some corrugated sheds, uninhabited – at nine-forty, and after a pause to let bones stop shaking, had departed within ten minutes. I trust nobody turned up subsequently and waited there, assuming the train was late; he would never have lasted out the week.

A dirt road runs beside the line, the main road from Croydon to Normanton and almost innocent of traffic. But at ten-thirty a Toyota shot past and stopped, and Mr Honey stopped also, reversed, and went back for a yarn with the family piled inside – parents, two barefoot sons and two dishevelled daughters. The outback code is not to pass someone without receiving a thumbs-up, or a wave, or a 'she'll be right mate'. In the cities of Australia and the West it would, of course, be the other way round: the train would observe the timetable punctually and forget about people. But in the bush they still prefer the spirit to the law.

Although the occasional plague of grasshoppers makes the rails slippery, Mr Honey says that most of the time there is not a great amount of variety *en route*; it would not be the Australian bush if there were. This line has no tunnels, no cuttings, no signals – no need if there's only one train. Anthills change in shape, from that of cones to Christmas puddings; in sandier soils there's more of one type of gum and less of another; occasionally a wild turkey flaps away. That's about it in this emptiest of continents.

How despondent therefore must the great Australian explorers have been on returning home after one of their journeys and reporting to their superiors about what they had found. 'Well, Carruthers' (for they were, for the most part, minor English gentry), the governor or surveyor-general would have said. 'Tell me, did you find the famous inland sea that we have long been seeking?'

'Er, no, sir.'

'Then you bring back news of some fine inland rivers that will irrigate pastures for our cattle?'

'No, sir. I'm sorry, sir.'

'In that case, Carruthers, even though you did not find water, you have discovered great ranges of mountains which we can add to the map?'

'No, sir, I'm afraid we found none.'

'Carruthers, your expedition lasted eighteen months and twelve days, and in that time you say you marched 2,395 miles. Do you dare stand here and tell me that you discovered absolutely nothing?'

'Well, sir, we did find a sort of creek, sir. But we had to call it Dry Creek. And we found a lake as well, sir, but it had dried up too, and we named it Lake Disappointment.'

'Carruthers!'

'Yes, sir?'

'You are dismissed.'

At eleven o'clock, well ahead of schedule, we approached the salt flats around the Norman River where Ludwig Leichhardt halted in 1845. He was forced to search for a crossing up-stream before he could proceed north-east through Arnhem Land, to arrive eventually near modern Darwin, successful but unsatisfied with his discoveries. A few miles away Burke and Wills later sought the sea, in order to prove they had traversed the continent from south to north. They too were disappointed. They never set eyes upon the sea: only the water's saltiness in the Gulf country provided evidence that they had effectively completed their crossing. 'It would have been well to say that we reached the sea,' wrote Burke, 'but we could not obtain a view of the open ocean, although we made every endeavour to do so.'

RM93 roared across the grey-brown waters of the Norman River, muddy and scrubby, unattractive for swimming. Its bridge is several feet higher than the road bridge alongside, which partly explains why the railway is maintained at all. That extra height keeps the train running, long after the road is flooded and impassable. Thus in the exceptional year of 1974, when the whole region was under water, nothing could move. But in a fairly typical wet season like 1981, when Normanton was cut off for eight weeks (except for its airfield), the train got out a fortnight before any car could. And the aviation fuel it brought back from Croydon was invaluable.

Normally the rail motor doesn't carry much more freight than Croydon's weekly supply of bread and meat, so it's this vital difference during the wet season which is the chief argument for keeping the train going. It might have psychological importance too: the Gulf Country people feel cut off as it is, without their trusty steel being taken from them.

On the Normanton side of the river the railway itself had a kind of psychological crisis back in 1887: it didn't know where it was going. It had to stop and wait on the banks of the Norman until the state parliament in Brisbane worked out what its role in life was meant to be. Initially – and this is not the least of the oddities about the Normanton–Croydon Railway – it was not intended to go to Croydon at all. It was originally destined for Cloncurry. Cloncurry boasted copper and gold, so the decision had originally been made, in 1886, to send the railway there. But that year Croydon boomed. Parliament scratched its head – perhaps the railway should not go to Cloncurry after all. Engineer Phillips thereupon came along with a convenient compromise which was accepted. He proposed constructing the first few miles as far as the Norman River, and then assessing the next stage in the light of the respective goldrushes to Croydon and Cloncurry. And by 1889 Croydon was still booming, so they sent the line there. But when Croydon ran out of workable gold, the line faced the axe. After the First World War it had to economise or close.

So staff were laid off and rolling stock reduced in a pattern that railways around the globe came to know: by the early 1920s the service was down to its present level of one journey each way per week. Moreover, a rail motor was introduced in 1921 – 'a small railcar fitted with a simple type oil engine'. It was meant for the use of the maintenance gang, but was soon found to be suitable for the public as well. The steam locomotives were left to disintegrate in sidings or in the yard at Normanton, where their skeletons are still scattered, while the primitive rail motor survives. Since 1929 all services have been by rail motor, and seldom has there been a demand for even a second carriage.

That afternoon a cloud no bigger than a man's hand formed away over the Gulf that was named after Pieter Carpentier. Towards evening the sky was blackened with clouds like bitumen. A horse cantered around a dusty field flicking its tail. A dust-devil, or willy-willy, scurried towards Normanton, agitating the red earth, as the fettlers' gang returned hastily down the track on their phut-phutting motor trolley to beat the storm home.

But rain did not fall. What sounded like rain drops on the tin roofs of Normanton was only the metal contracting. Then the sky went orange with the dust-storm. Orange earth and orange sky became one, advancing together to drown the land. It was the Aborigines' Snake-man on his last great journey, the Snake-man who made the clouds out of marsupial fur and eagle-hawk down while he travelled north and south. He also left many lightning rods, which shot through the distant sky, and this lightning lights a path for the Aborigines who are roaming the Australian bush and making a journey in a dream-spirit.

13
Townsville to Julia Creek

'We could not sense any bitterness or grudge. Rather there was pride and something close to rejoicing that their loved ones had died in a service they enjoyed so much.'

(The Country Fire Authority chaplain, after speaking to the families of twelve volunteer firefighters who died when their fire trucks were trapped at Upper Beaconsfield, March 1983)

'THE WRATH OF GOD FROM HEAVEN UN-LEASHED!!!' read one of the hand-outs on a stencilled sheet. Townsville, like most mainline stations up the Queensland coast, is stacked with boxes full of religious pamphlets, magazines and leaflets. This most lurid of them went on:

Prior to the DARWIN CYCLONE DISASTER, *CHRIST warned* Australians to *REPENT, BELIEVE* and *OBEY HIM*, or the above DISASTERS would begin to be unleashed from Heaven against the Un-Godliness of Sinners who refuse to obey THE TRUTH!!! The warning went out week after week from Townsville, then – as people laughed and mocked – *DARWIN WAS WIPED OFF THE MAP!!!*

Millenarianism is strong in Australia, not so strong perhaps as in America but stronger than in Britain. It is particularly prevalent on the coasts of Queensland and northern New South Wales, where communes, peddling the weed or Dianetics or fundamentalist religion, flourish in the hothouse climate, offering antidotes to what is arguably the most materialist of cultures.

I was flicking through these pamphlets, waiting for the railcar to Charters Towers, when a youngish, clean-shaven man came over and said, 'Hi. I'm Stephen.' He had a book with him about Nostradamus. Nostradamus, given a certain tendency to over-simplify complex issues, was big in some parts of Australia. I headed off down the platform, but when the railcar came in it turned out to consist of two cars only and Stephen quickly homed in again.

'Hi. I'm Stephen.' He sat down opposite, shifting in his seat. He was trying to get something off his chest, struggling like the railcar up the Great Dividing Range. 'That's Reid River, or meant to be. Should be full this time of year. I'm an engineer in Telecom by the way, pleased to meet you. That's the Burdekin, should be full too at this stage of the Wet. But it's real dry . . .'

He leaned forward. 'Have you ever considered there could be a drought in your life? Don't you feel you're like one of those fields out there, crying out for the rain that is Jesus?'

Then he was going on about bankcards. One of the pamphlets had warned: 'Your Commonwealth bankcard – ETERNAL DOOM' which, so Stephen said, had nothing to do with high monthly interest rates. 'The Countdown commenced on January 1, 1973' apparently, and one of the signs of the last days is that everyone, except for true Christians, will be forced to accept a trading mark to buy or sell. This boiled down to bankcards. For if you look at your friendly piece of plastic in a certain way – and read into it what you want – you can see 666, Antichrist's number. So the fact that most Australians have bankcards is a certain proof that the last days have come, although Stephen was not quite clear about why God, having chosen Israel as the scene of His earlier revelations, should have switched to the shopping plazas of Australia for His messianic return. But there you go.

According to one of America's leading cult psychologists, much involved in Jonestown, the members of these charismatic cults are hard to identify because they often lead double lives – upstanding citizens one minute, then slipping the old indoctrination cassette tape in. Stephen fitted that bill. He switched from the rational, talking about Telecom and Charters Towers as a former gold town, over to the brainwash and back again. I was lucky the journey only took two hours.

Charters Towers is more varied than most country towns because it has developed – since its gold ran out – as the centre for boarding schools in the north-east of Australia. But it still has roots in the surrounding cattle stations and I spent that evening in one of those ringers' pubs where the men come to blow their pay cheques after months *sans* grog and women in the bush. Australian pubs trace their spiritual descent back to Scottish pubs, particularly those Glaswegian ones where the nearest they come to furnishings are the bars on the windows, and carpets are not commonly found. One of the most characteristic sounds indeed of outback Australia, the one I'll recall most nostalgically, is the noise which comes to you in the early morning as the yard man with mop and bucket sluices down the floors.

Half a dozen male customers were lined up at the bar, and Shirl. Every man kept his can cool in his own plastic container, and a pile of change alongside. Most were in felt hats, smoking. Shirl was walking around, lurching a bit, wanting someone to talk to. The other men looked as if they had been talked to sufficiently. Slowly she worked her way round the semi-circular bar to where I was standing.

'Hi, I'm a gin. I know I'm a gin, look at my nose, see? And I'm proud of it. But why do people have to tell me every time I see 'em: "Hello, gin, how are you goin', gin?" Why do they always have to tell me I'm a gin?'

'Perhaps because they feel insecure and need someone to look down on?' I suggested. 'Most people seem to need someone to look down on.'

Then she paused. ''Ere, I like talking to you. I feel I could tell you things, get them off my chest. How about we get some marihuana and a guitar and go somewhere – I know someone who's got a nice girl for you. Come on, let's get some "mara" and some beers . . .'

Before I could weigh up the attractions of this proposition, a little cold water was poured by the woman behind the bar. 'If her old man sees you with her,' she told me matter-of-factly, 'he'll kill you.'

This friendly bush telegraph wasn't wrong: 'He is a pig,' Shirl agreed. 'See that there – nine stitches in my forehead, and five here. I was married to a Dane once, but I live with him now, the pig. He's English. But you're all right. Come on, let's get some beers . . .'

'I used to be a barmaid for eighteen years in Tennant Creek,' Shirl perked up. 'I've had three nervous breakdowns, been in the nut-house in Townsville and gone to London. You think I'm bull-shitting. No, I've seen London, mate, fair dinkum. For two days.' She smiled, quite handsome, before her head slumped over the counter. True, she had an Aborigine's nose but her skin was no darker than many a bushman's.

'Oh Lord/won't you buy me/a Mercedes Benz': she lifted up her head and sang – well. One of her two heroes was the England cricketer Bob Willis, the other Bob Dylan. 'I used to sing at parties, and they said I should go in for the Country and Western Festival here in Charters . . . but it's my nerves, I couldn't control myself before a performance . . .' Shirl slumped again. The ceiling fan ruffled the back of her hair. The half-dozen around the bar were silently absorbed in drinking-up time.

'She comes in here about twice a week, after he's bashed her up.' The woman of the friendly warning behind the bar turned out to be the publican as well. 'Her husband's banned from here: he's a *real* pig. But there's quite a few workers, mind you, who come in here at five o'clock, drink till nine, and go home and give the wife one with the back of their hand.'

The publican herself was fair-skinned for a bush girl: she said it was because she, and her Alsatian, had run the pub for over a year and scarcely been outdoors in that time. Her blonde hair was long and had been swung over one shoulder. She was perceptive too.

'The ringers who come here have just worked for three months or so out on a station, and they arrive in town to blow their cheque, often two thousand dollars or more. They hand it over to me straight away and get drunk, so drunk they fall off their stool, and I have to get them put to bed. Next morning they'll get drunk again, totally drunk, and so on for about a week, after which they'll go off and see their wife in town – or more likely the woman they live with and illegitimate kid. But only then, after being in the bush all those months and getting drunk here for a week.

'Yes, there are still a few pubs like this one where they get their mail sent to, and you have to help them read their letters, fill in their forms, act as their solicitor and bank and post office and so on. They hand over their whole pay-cheque and you could steal the lot, though I don't swindle a cent because they're so trusting; they're really neat people. They aren't violent when drunk, these ringers, even if they might look like it. They just fall over and collapse on the floor.

'And when they've finished their holiday, I hand them whatever's left and that's not much after the grog and women, so they just carry on. The majority of them must be illiterate – when automatic telephones replaced the turn-handle ones, about three-quarters couldn't work out how to use them – but I like doing things for them. My parents ran a pub and I guess it's one thing I'm good at.'

Closing time was at hand. The publican put her arm round Shirl and led her to the door, pointed her in the direction for home and said, 'Take care.'

The original pattern of railways in Queensland was for them to head inland from various ports on the east coast: from Brisbane to bush towns like Goondiwindi (just over the border from Boggabilla), from Cairns to Forsayth, from Rockhampton to Longreach and Winton (where Qantas started, and so dusty they say that kangaroos there jump backwards), and from Townsville to Mount Isa. Only later were the coastal ports linked up by a north-south line from Cairns to Brisbane.

The Great Northern Railway first left Townsville for Charters Towers when the latter's goldrush began in the 1880s. It was pushed on to Julia Creek by 1908, then to 'the Curry' and 'the Isa' as railwaymen call Cloncurry and Mount Isa: 603 miles of single, wobbly, pioneer track the condition of which had brought the trains to a near stand-still by the early sixties. It was then decided that Mount Isa's proven reserves of copper, lead and zinc were sufficient to justify a new line, a massive project which cost fifty-four million dollars. Ore now is taken to the coast for refining; so are cattle after the Wet for their own brand of refining. So from Charters Towers I took another Mixed Goods heading west, for the final stage to Julia Creek.

At Prairie – a handful of bungalows and a wooden church on stilts, visited once a month by man and maybe no more often by God – the bush gave way to plains, or prairie. Shortly before it we passed a few scattered gum trees, the trunks of which had been burnt black by fire. But their leaves had turned a russet colour, so that this copse was like a group of thin chorus girls, auburn-haired and dressed in black stockings – like Julia Matthews as she might have been dressed, waiting for news of Burke back in Melbourne.

We came to another tiny township, Marathon. No mountains look on this Marathon, only the sun, and Marathon looks on nothing. Now the land was yet more arid, dryness having given way to drought. While the Mixed Goods halted for half an hour I sat on the tailboard and the unwatchable orb throbbed overhead. More corpses lay alongside the road, of kangaroos that had strayed too close, looking for the last remaining tufts of grass.

Moving off again the train headed further west towards Julia Creek. Earth was crumbled dust and the plains as featureless as they were flat and waterless, except for a kind of acacia. Spread over western Queensland by the flooding of 1974, they are locally known as prickly trees; and they have made it difficult for the cattle-mustering to be done by horse, because the cattle hide under their branches. Even when helicopters were introduced for mustering, the cattle rapidly became accustomed to the whirring blades and continued hiding under the branches. So here they go round the prickly tree, the prickly tree . . .

The Mixed Goods rolled on to Julia Creek through desert

aridity. Still no rain came from a sky blooded by the evening's dust. But lightning began to carve it up with forking 'Ys': the Snake-man was on the move again, silently. Then sheet lightning, caused by the female Jadangal: the Jadangal have lights on the insides of their thighs which flicker when they dance, thereby lighting another path for those Aborigines who are making a journey in dream-spirit.

And as the train finally approached Julia Creek, a small settlement in the vastness of the prairie and with lightning flashing round about, the pamphlet's Wrath of God was indeed from Heaven Unleashed upon Australia. Around Melbourne and Adelaide bushfires broke out that were as ferocious as any during this century. They caused the deaths of seventy-two people. They also sparked a revival of the old Australian virtues of generosity and mateship.

Victoria, along with California and the French Riviera, is one of the world's most dangerous areas for fire: its dryness, the combustible quality of native trees – especially Victorian eucalypts – and the strength of local winds are the intensifying factors. Fanned by these winds the bushfires, started by spontaneous combustion or power lines touching against trees or even by vandalism, built up to a heat which was calculated to be equal to that of an atom bomb.

Eight thousand people were made homeless and forty-six incinerated in Victoria, twenty-six more in South Australia. Twelve volunteer firefighters went to defend a house at the top of a wooded hill in Upper Beaconsfield outside Melbourne. They parked their two fire trucks halfway up the hill and made their stand. It is said that you can survive a bushfire if you stay inside your house or car, or truck, but these twelve either died beneath their vehicle or were burnt to cinders against the bank of the hill.

About 15,000 volunteers fought the Victorian fires alongside police and other officials, but they could do little to stop them spreading like napalm moving at thirty miles an hour. They might spray a chemical retardant from planes or bulldoze the potential fuel of the forests, but the only effective way is answering fire with fire, by backburning to clear a break in the wooded hills.

In the days that followed the generosity of Australians was demonstrated as amply as their courage had been. Within a week ten million dollars had been donated by public and private subscription. Amongst the latter came a cheque for two thousand dollars from a nineteen-year-old girl who had been saving to go overseas. It had been posted with a note that said: 'After witnessing the devastating fires in Upper Beaconsfield, etc., I think you could use my savings for far better things than I ever could. I'm only sorry I haven't got more to give.'

A matter of days later nature struck again. Torrents rained down on land that had become too parched to absorb water, first around Adelaide and then through the eastern states. Creeks, having been dry for years, ran ten feet high and more. Cattle, having starved, were drowned; sheep were bogged down by the weight of water in their fleeces. And again the Australian spirit was displayed in innumerable feats of generosity and heroism that Burke would have been proud of, or diver Hughes in Coolgardie, or Joe Harman in fiction, or the men of Zeehan and Queenstown, or the publican in Charters Towers.

That spirit is still willing. And while the most suburbanised of peoples may be understandably absorbed in their daily domestic cares, while excellence may tend to be pursued in sport and neglected elsewhere, while enjoyment of the good life may sometimes be taken to excess, this generosity of spirit can counterbalance them all. It is a spirit of humanity and provided it is displayed so as to include all Australians in future, I'm sure 'she'll be right'.